W9-DCJ-804

ST. MARY'S HIGH SCHOOL

HEIDEGGER

A BEGINNER'S GUIDE

HEIDEGGER

A BEGINNER'S GUIDE

MICHAEL WATTS

Hodder & Stoughton

A MEMBER OF THE HODDER HEADLINE GROUP

Orders: please contact Bookpoint Ltd, 78 Milton Park, Abingdon, Oxon OX14 4TD. Telephone: (44) 01235 400400, Fax: (44) 01235 400500. Lines are open from 9.00–6.00, Monday to Saturday, with a 24-hour message answering service. Email address: orders@bookpoint.co.uk

British Library Cataloguing in Publication Data
A catalogue record for this title is available from The British Library

ISBN 0 340 80324 X

First published 2001
Impression number   10 9 8 7 6 5 4 3 2 1
Year 2007 2006 2005 2004 2003 2002

Copyright © 2001 Michael Watts

All rights reserved. No part of this publication may be reproduced or transmitted in any form or by any means, electronic or mechanical, including photocopy, recording, or any information storage and retrieval system, without permission in writing from the publisher or under licence from the Copyright Licensing Agency Limited. Further details of such licences (for reprographic reproduction) may be obtained from the Copyright Licensing Agency Limited, of 90 Tottenham Court Road, London, W1P 9HE.

Cover photo from Corbis Images.
Typeset by Transet Limited, Coventry, England.
Printed in Great Britain for Hodder & Stoughton Educational, a division of Hodder Headline Plc, 338 Euston Road, London NW1 3BH by Cox & Wyman, Reading, Berks.

CONTENTS

FOREWORD   viii
PREFACE   ix

CHAPTER 1: THE LIFE OF HEIDEGGER   1
The roots   1
The influences of his environment   1
Education   2
Heidegger's academic career   3
Heidegger and Nazism   7
The post-war years   8

CHAPTER 2: THE MEANING OF LIFE –
THE QUESTION OF BEING   10
The ontological 'error' of Western philosophy   11
Heidegger's fundamental ontology   11
An argument against Heidegger's approach   12
Heidegger's response to nihilism   13
Heidegger's vocabulary   13
'Being' and 'being'   14
Ourselves as the initial subject-matter of the inquiry   15
Time as the horizon of Being   17
Being and Time   18
The Nothing   19
Why is there something rather than Nothing?   21
The significance of unanswerable questions   22

CHAPTER 3: THE CENTRAL CONCEPTS OF *BEING* AND *TIME* 24
Dasein – ourselves as the starting point   24
The *a priori* structure of *Dasein*   25

The world   26
Dasein's Being-in-the-world   27
Dasein's ordinary, everyday existence   27
Ready-to-hand and present-at-hand   28
Heidegger 'equipment totality'   29
Space and time   31
Being-with-others   32
Dasein's throwness   33
Inauthenticity: the 'they-self'   34
Inauthenticity: falling   35
Moods   38
Understanding   41
Interpretation   42
Meaning   43
Anxiety   43
Care   46

CHAPTER 4: BEING-TOWARDS-DEATH   49
The 'afterlife' issue   50
Heidegger's 'facts of life' and death   50
Death as a possibility   51

CHAPTER 5: CONSCIENCE, GUILT AND AUTHENTICITY   54
Conscience   54
Guilt   55
Authenticity   56

CHAPTER 6: THE 'TRUTH OF *ALETHEIA*' AND LANGUAGE   61
Traditional concepts of truth   61
Heidegger's truth of *aletheia*   62

Contents

Heidegger's concept of language   66
The emptiness of everyday langauge   66
The language of Being   67
Ancient Greek and German   68
Talk – the basis of language   69
Language – our primary access to Being   70
The silent 'saying' of the world   70
The language of poetry   71

CHAPTER 7: TAO, ZEN AND HEIDEGGER   73
Taoism and Heidegger   73
Zen and Heidegger   75

CHAPTER 8: HEIDEGGER ON TECHNOLOGY   79
Enframing: the 'mind-set' of technology   80
Techne, poiesis and the *essence* of technology   83
Enframing: danger or source of awareness?   84
Heidegger's response to technology   87

FURTHER READING   90
GLOSSARY   91
INDEX   96

Foreword

Michael Watts gives an exceptionally clear and readable account of Being and Time, while also performing the difficult feat of weaving this into an account of Heidegger's later writings. He provides valuable guidance for the beginner through the complexities of Heidegger's thought and much of interest for those who are already 'on the way'.

If you knew this would be the last day of your life, how would you spend it? Your answer says a lot about who you are' (p. 49). One answer to Michael Watts' question might be that I would write a Foreword to his book. But I have no idea whether this is the answer I would give, let alone whether it is the correct answer or even if there is a correct answer. (The question is insufficiently specific. How much time has been allowed for the preparation that my preferred activity might require?) Suppose that I would give this answer, even that it is the right answer. Why should it say more about me than any other day's activity? At best, its message is ambiguous. Am I motivated by regard for Heidegger or for Watts, by respect for the literary obligation I have assumed, or even by indifference to my imminent demise? Here, then, I disagree with Watts. But I am grateful to him for these, and other, thoughts provoked by his book.

Michael Inwood
Professor of Philosophy, Trinity College, Oxford

PREFACE

In the *Encyclopaedia Britannica*, the opening paragraph on Martin Heidegger reads: 'German philosopher, counted among the main exponents of twentieth-century Existentialism. He was an original thinker, a critic of technological society, a leading ontologist of his time, and an influence on the younger generation of continental European cultural personalities.'

Yet in the history of Western thought since the time of Socrates, no one has been judged in such a wide-ranging and extreme manner as Heidegger.

Bertrand Russell allocated a mere five lines to Heidegger in his *A History of Western Philosophy* (1946), and described his work as being 'eccentric and obscure – Existentialist psychology masquerading as logic'. The analytic philosopher A.J. Ayer labelled him 'a charlatan', and Roger Scruton, a conservative British philosopher and author, described Heidegger's most important work *Being and Time* as 'formidably difficult – unless it is utter nonsense, in which case it is laughably easy'.

In contrast to this, the eminent American philosopher and political theorist Professor Richard Rorty describes Heidegger, in his *Philosophy and the Mirror of Nature* (1979), as being one of the three most important philosophers of the twentieth century (along with Dewey and Wittgenstein). Other equally respected academics regard him as *the* most important European philosopher of the twentieth century – one of that small number of elite Western thinkers that includes Plato, Aristotle and Descartes.

Heidegger's influence is indisputable, and his impact on modern life is widespread – in philosophy, literature, poetry, theatre, sociology and even architecture. He has been described as: a German Idealist Philosopher concerned with fundamental questions of death, time, and the *Angst* or anxiety of daily life; a master scholar and interpreter of history's most influential philosophers; a 'language mystic' –

involved more deeply than any other philosopher with the influence that language exerts on human thought. He was an invaluable contributor to the evolution of the method of philosophy known as phenomenology, which was developed by his teacher Edmund Husserl. In addition, Heidegger was the main influence behind the work of Jean-Paul Sartre, and thus contributed greatly to the development of twentieth-century Existentialism. He has even been regarded as a theological academic who has provided an excellent philosophical basis for modern Christian thought. The most recurrent view of Heidegger, however, is that he is ultimately a 'philosopher of Being', who pursued the question of the 'meaning of Being' relentlessly until death finally ended his quest.

Heidegger demonstrated remarkable ecological awareness for his time. He expressed strong concern over, and was highly opposed to, many components of the modern industrial society, with its overemphasis on technology and mass culture, and he spoke strongly against the mistreatment of livestock and the abuse of the planet's resources. With superb clairvoyance he prophetically warned of the coming destruction of the environment that would lead to planetary-ecological crises.

There is undoubtedly a very dark side to Heidegger which has been the greatest cause of controversy surrounding his life – his involvement with Nazism and the political forces, if any, that can be read into his philosophy. He has often been described as a German 'redneck' and a gullible, self-important Nazi and yet there are still academics who insist he was in fact a covert critic of Nazism.

There is also a private side to Heidegger that is still not known, as most of his personal, private papers remain locked away in the German Literary Archive in Marbach, where access has been strictly limited.

Finally, there is a yet-to-be-discovered Heidegger, in the form of a vast amount of philosophical material he wrote that still needs to be edited before it can be published.

All these various facets of Heidegger's philosophy and personality are tainted with ambiguity, many seem incompatible and all of them are controversial. One wonders what sort of background might have contributed to such a complex, diverse personality. This book will allow the reader to form his or her own informed answer to this open-ended question.

To make it easier for the reader, clear explanations of Heidegger's innovative and often obscure use of language have been provided throughout the text, and attention has been paid to locating the middle ground between the highly varied explanations of his thought. Enormous attention to detail has gone into making sure that his philosophical concepts are explained as clearly and unambiguously as possible. Complete newcomers to philosophy should now be able to understand the central ideas of arguably the most complex and obscure of all philosophers.

The Life of Heidegger

THE ROOTS
The small town of Messkirch in the Black Forest region of Baden-Wurttemberg, southwest Germany is the home of St. Martin's, a small, quiet Catholic church. In its hilltop graveyard there is a tombstone inscribed 'Martin Heidegger, 1889–1976'. It is marked with a star, recalling a line written by the philosopher in 1947: 'To think is to confine yourself to a single thought that one day stands still like a star in the world's sky.'

Heidegger was born in Messkirch – a pious, conservative agricultural town – to a poor lower-middle class, devout Catholic family. The church employed his father Friedrich as bell-ringer, gravedigger and caretaker of the vestments and sacred vessels.

But are such details really relevant to understanding his philosophy? It seems reasonable to answer 'yes' to this question, though Heidegger's own views on this matter are clearly ambiguous. In 1955 during a memorial address in Messkirch, Heidegger claimed: 'The greater the master, the more completely his person vanishes behind his work.' Yet later on in the same speech he quotes from a local poet: 'We are like plants which – whether we like to admit it to ourselves or not, must with our roots rise out of the earth in order to bloom in the ether and to bear fruit.' Like this speech, Heidegger's life and philosophy were full of contradiction.

THE INFLUENCES OF HIS ENVIRONMENT
The society in which he lived made him especially sympathetic towards the traditional German country lifestyle. He was subjected to an atmosphere saturated with Christian doctrines of sin and redemption, and was part of a social class ruled by centuries-old routines of hard

daily labour. He felt a part of the cultivated farmland and especially loved to hike and ski through the Black Forest landscape. These early life experiences of nature, handicraft, the struggle to find the right way to be, and guilt, all became focuses for his later philosophical thought.

This background simultaneously made him antagonistic towards modern city life, with its cosmopolitanism, liberal democracy and its excessive concern for technology and productivity. Indeed, in 1933 he refused to leave Freiburg to teach in Berlin, explaining that his 'philosophical work ... belongs right in the midst of the "peasants" work'.

EDUCATION

From an early age Heidegger displayed a keen interest in religion and clearly seemed destined for the priesthood. In 1903 he received a scholarship to attend the *Gymnasium* (high school) in Konstanz where he lived in a Catholic boarding house. Three years later he transferred to another *Gymnasium* in Freiburg. The church continued to provide him with free board and lodging, whilst he simultaneously trained for the priesthood at the Freiburg Jesuit Seminary. It was here, in the summer of 1907, that Martin Heidegger, now a seventeen-year-old high school student, received a book from Dr. Conrad Grober, a pastor and paternal friend. This book marked the start of his lifelong relationship with philosophy. Written by the Catholic thinker Franz Brentano and entitled *On the Manifold Meaning of Being according to Aristotle* (1862), it was by Heidegger's own account, 'the chief help and guide of my first awkward attempts to penetrate into philosophy'.

In 1909 he left the high school to become a Jesuit novice, at the Society of Jesus in Tisis, Austria, only to leave a couple of weeks later as a result of severe chest pains that were attributed to heart trouble. His interest in religion remained strong however, and for the next two years a Church scholarship paid for his studies at the theological seminary of Albert-Ludwig University in Freiburg, where he studied Catholic theology and medieval Christian philosophy in preparation for the priesthood.

It was at this time that he encountered his next major philosophical influence – a book entitled *On Being: An Outline of Ontology* (1896). It was written by Carl Braig, a professor who taught him systematic theology at Freiburg University. This book established Heidegger's deep commitment to what he considered to be the single most important question of existence: 'What is Being?' The attempt to provide answers to this became Heidegger's central preoccupation – an obsession that gripped him until his death.

In 1911, owing to asthma and further heart problems, he abandoned his training for the priesthood and transferred instead from the seminary training to become, officially, a student of philosophy. Though he never lost his interest in theology, it became far less central to his life and academic pursuits.

He now immersed himself in the works of Aristotle, whilst also studying mathematics, and the human and natural sciences. He was also attracted to writers who explored the extremes of emotion and human experience: Nietzsche, Dostoyevsky and Kierkegaard. Most important of all were two thinkers whom Heidegger had studied for several years, Wilhelm Dilthey (1833–1911) and Edmund Husserl (1859–1939). Heidegger's later philosophy was in many senses a creative combination of the ideas and methods from both these men.

HEIDEGGER'S ACADEMIC CAREER
After receiving his doctorate in 1913, and completing a thesis in 1915 that gave him the right to teach in German universities, he began lecturing in psychology at Freiburg under the guidance of Edmund Husserl, a Jewish Professor who held the chair of psychology at the university. He soon became his most trusted assistant. Heidegger later came to play a crucial role in the development of Phenomenology, a movement in philosophy that was led by Husserl. The personal relationship between Husserl and Heidegger was a quasi-parental one – Mrs Husserl was reported on occasion to have introduced Heidegger to others as her husband's 'phenomenological child'.

He was conscripted in 1915, but after two months discharged on grounds of health. Early in 1917 he again went into the army, assigned to military postal services. Being stationed in Freiburg, he used to complete his day's work by returning to the university to conduct his lectures and seminars. In this same year he married a Protestant, Elfriede Petri. In 1918 he was sent to a meteorological station on the western front near Verdun, where he served until the Armistice (he never saw combat). In 1919 and 1920 his two sons, Jorg and Hermann, were born. Shortly after the birth of his first son, he wrote a letter to a friend in which he said that various philosophical insights had made Catholicism unacceptable to him. Like Edmund Husserl, Heidegger strongly believed that philosophy is only properly done when a thinker frees himself of all theological assumptions.

As a lecturer, Heidegger was soon recognized as a teacher of amazing brilliance. He interpreted, with mesmerizing passionate intensity and startling originality of insight, philosophers such as Plato, Descartes, Kant and Hegel, and his courses on phenomenology, on Aristotle, and on the human being in its world of everyday experience earned him the reputation of being the 'hidden king' of philosophy. He often used a method that, although popular today, was unheard of at the time. He would guide his students towards a deep understanding of the core of a philosopher's thinking by having them study just two or three carefully selected pages of the philosopher's work. Through this approach, they often achieved a greater depth of understanding in a matter of months, than others could gain during years of study. He exuded the energy of a revolutionary thinker who was so filled with the passion of his thought that he hypnotized his audience. Until Heidegger, people had been accustomed to the old opposition of reason versus passion, spirit versus life – he shocked his audiences by proving this wrong with a fiery enthusiasm that combined with incredible philosophical perception. His students claimed that it seemed as if he cast a spell over his listeners that had a transformative effect on their consciousness.

Not only were Heidegger's philosophical concepts and style of teaching distinctive, but even his manner of dress. Early in his teaching career he adopted a unique style, designed personally for him by a well-known local painter. It was nicknamed 'the existential outfit'. Though one student described it as having the 'modest magnificence of a farmer dressed up for Sunday', it turned out to resemble the sinister uniform later worn by Hitler's SA troops.

Heidegger's Associate Professorship

In 1922, as a result of his insightful, creative interpretations of Aristotle, Heidegger was offered, and accepted, the position of Associate Professor of Philosophy at Marburg University. There he drew a following of students who travelled from the four corners of Europe to study with him. In spite of the fact that he had never published any works he soon became widely known throughout Germany as a genius and radical thinker, simply by the force of his teaching. It was here, in 1924, that he began an intimate and enduring relationship with a highly gifted eighteen-year-old Jewish philosophy student, Hannah Arendt.

Being and Time and his full Professorship

In January 1926, the authorities in Berlin rejected the University of Marburg's proposal to grant Heidegger a full professorship, in view of his 'not very large literary accomplishments'. Later that year at Edmund Husserl's 67th birthday party, Heidegger presented his work *Being and Time,* which he had dedicated to Husserl. Although it was not anywhere near complete, Husserl arranged for its publication on 8 April, 1927. Heidegger suddenly achieved international renown and a full professorship at Marburg University.

In 1928, he was invited back to Freiburg to occupy the Chair of Philosophy formerly held by the now-retired Edmund Husserl. Within a few years *Being and Time* won recognition in many philosophical circles as an epoch-making work of twentieth-century European philosophy – it was and still remains undoubtedly Heidegger's most famous and most influential work. The difficulties posed by its philosophical originality and highly obscure style made understanding its major claims an incredibly difficult enterprise, even for a philosophically trained reader.

In spite of this, the book was acclaimed as a deep and important work, not only in German-speaking countries, but also in Latin countries where Phenomenology was already well known. It strongly influenced Jean-Paul Sartre in France and the **Existentialism** movement, and despite Heidegger's protestations he was classed, on the strength of this book, as the leading atheistic Existentialist. However, it did not receive the same warm reception in the English-speaking world, and its influence there was negligible for several decades.

His banishment from Anglo–American philosophy

On the occasion of his inauguration as professor at Freiburg, Heidegger delivered one of his most famous lectures: 'What is **Metaphysics?**' This powerful exploration of anxiety and its relation to nothingness became a key text for Existentialists, as well as the subject of great controversy. It was also largely responsible for Heidegger's exclusion from the world of Anglo-American philosophy.

There were two statements in this lecture responsible for this reaction. The first, 'Nothingness itself nothings', sounded to many philosophers like complete nonsense. The second was, 'The idea of "logic" itself disintegrates in the turbulence of a more original questioning'. Many philosophers at the time believed (and still do) that philosophy should express facts in an objective, logical, scientific manner – there should be no ambiguous propositions. In contrast to this, Heidegger's statements seemed wildly irrational and therefore, amongst English-speaking philosophers, his work was not taken seriously.

His rejection of the Chair of Philosophy in Berlin

In 1930, he rejected the offer of a Chair in Berlin, as he disliked the noise of big cities, their social and cultural lifestyle and the cosmopolitan elegance of the German intellectual aristocracy. He had no interest in a social life revolving round professorial dinner tables and other such gatherings, preferring instead to spend his time with his wife and two young sons, leading the provincial lifestyle typical of southern Germany with its small towns and rough, unspoiled landscape.

Most of his writing was done in this environment in the modest mountain cottage that he built in 1923 above the town of Todtnauberg in the Black Forest. He liked the country way of living, where he could take breaks from his writing in order to immerse himself in simple physical activities, such as chopping wood or cross-country skiing.

HEIDEGGER AND NAZISM

In Germany, the years between 1918 and 1933 were characterized by economic troubles and political confusion. On 2 August 1934, Hitler was proclaimed 'Leader of the German Empire'.

Up until the end of the 1920s, Heidegger had been virtually apolitical, but by the early 1930s he had already developed a strong respect for Nazism. In April 1933, Heidegger was unanimously elected Rector of the University of Freiburg and a couple of weeks after this he became an official member of the Nazi Party.

Heidegger's lectures on 'Being' became increasingly polluted with Nazi political sentiment, culminating in his speech on the eve of the Reichstag elections in November 1933, when he spoke out in open support of Hitlerian policies that had been responsible for Germany's withdrawal from the League of Nations.

As a rector he co-operated with the new regime by helping to synchronize the administration, faculty and student bodies of German universities with the Nazi Party political policies. But in April 1934 he resigned from his position owing to conflicts with the faculty and with party officials. He did however retain his Nazi membership card, even though he was no longer an active member of the party.

Heidegger's downfall

In 1944, Heidegger was drafted into the German Home Guard in Freiburg to help dig anti-tank ditches. In December, after Freiburg was bombed, he fled to Messkirch. In 1945 the Allies bombed Messkirch and French forces occupied Freiburg – Heidegger returned to stand before the De-Nazification Commission two months after Germany's final collapse.

The investigation concluded that he was guilty of various political crimes, and he was barred from teaching until 1949. He emerged from the proceedings a broken man. In 1946, probably owing to the stress and humiliation caused by the interrogatory questioning by the commission, he suffered a nervous breakdown and spent three weeks in a sanatorium in Badenweiler to recuperate.

THE POST-WAR YEARS

Heidegger's career in writing and lecturing soon recovered, but in the years after the war his publications were mostly revised versions of his lectures. During the 1950s and 1960s, though he travelled on a few lecture tours to France, Greece, Switzerland and around Germany, he never remained away from his Black Forest origins for long.

After his retirement in 1959, Heidegger left the university environment to spend most of his remaining life as a recluse at Todtnauberg, attempting to live in the solitude of his Black Forest mountain refuge in a way that embodied the values of his philosophy.

In a 1966 interview with the well-known German magazine *Der Spiegel,* (which was published, by agreement, after his death) he attempted to justify his conduct during the Nazi era. The fact that after the war, and even during this interview, he never openly apologized for his involvement with the Nazis, nor spoke of the atrocities they committed against the Jews and other Europeans, has shocked and confused everyone including his admirers. This refusal to discuss the Holocaust has infamously become known as 'Heidegger's Silence'.

In 1974 he assisted in the preparation of a *Collected Edition* of his works, which aimed to include his earlier publications as well as transcripts of all his lectures. His wish was that all the thoughts he had ever expressed in his publications and lectures would be preserved for posterity. The first volume of this edition was published in 1975. When completed, it will eventually consist of about 100 volumes. To date, only around 55 have been published.

Heidegger worked consistently until the end, when on the morning of 26 May, 1976, he died at his home in Freiburg.

2 The meaning of life – The Question of Being

The most important and persistent view of Heidegger is of a pioneering thinker who was concerned first and foremost with investigating the significance of the fundamental condition of all existence, which he called **Being**. The study of Being is known as **ontology**, and it has been around since the time of its birth in Greece in the 5th century BC, when thinkers such as Anaximander, Heraclitus, and Parmenides became intrigued by the seemingly inexplicable fact of existence. Heidegger noticed, however, that in Western philosophy since the time of Plato, and in all the sciences after Aristotle, hardly any attention has been focused directly on this fundamental mystery of life – the fact that there actually *is* a world and a universe rather than nothing at all. Consequently he saw the history of Western philosophy as rooted in a 'forgetting of Being' that has resulted in a gradual disintegration of values, incessant consumerism and technological domination.

Plato, and all the philosophers who came after him, made the grave mistake of adopting a 'theoretical stance' for their interpretation of Being. This created an artificial but fundamental rift between the isolated subject or 'mind' and an independently existing realm of objects, and caused what Heidegger called a 'splitting asunder of the phenomena', which has blinded most humans to the indivisibility and fundamental unity of Being.

As a result, the field of ontology has largely been characterized by an almost exclusive preoccupation with things in existence and the facts connected with them (which Heidegger calls **ontic** knowledge) – in other words, that which exists as a *consequence* of Being. This approach to ontology merely provides information *about* entities in the world and their characteristics (measurements, similarities and differences etc.)

without any regard for, or interest in the primordial fact of their Being (existence) – in other words, where they actually *came from*. The term **primordial**, which Heidegger uses frequently, refers to *that which is prior to everything and which therefore cannot be derived from anything else.*

THE ONTOLOGICAL 'ERROR' OF WESTERN PHILOSOPHY

But why did Western metaphysics forget Being? Why has it ignored the fundamental difference between Being and beings? According to Heidegger, the answer traces back to the Greek word for 'being', which is *parousia*. This word was ambiguous. The primary meaning was 'being' in the infinitive sense of 'to be', but it was also sometimes used to refer to 'being' in the nominal sense of 'substance', or 'a Supreme Being'. Unfortunately, although the earliest philosophers chose the former meaning, Plato and those after him chose the latter interpretations of this word – 'supreme being' or 'substance'. This resulted in a movement away from a radical 'thinking on Being' towards a search for the meaning of Being in some ultimate principle or 'divine agent'. For Plato, this took the form of what he termed the *idea*. Aristotle saw *substance* as the fundamental source of Being. Descartes proclaimed the source of Being was rooted in *God* and the *thinking subject* and Heidegger's teacher, Edmund Husserl, explained Being in terms of *pure consciousness*.

However, Heidegger considered that any search whatsoever for an *origin* of Being – whether in some type of substance, or in a transcendental super-Being (God) – was an evasion of the fundamental question of Being. He asserted that paths which argued a religious basis to Being were invalid, and he called them **onto-theologies.**

HEIDEGGER'S FUNDAMENTAL ONTOLOGY

Heidegger's ontology in *Being and Time* was a revolution – it established an entirely new way of thinking which differed radically from all the previous systems of ontological thinking.

The pre-Heideggerian approaches to ontology are based upon the attempt to question Being 'ontically'. These systems study what kinds of things exist and how to characterize them: Does God exist? Does freedom exist? Are body and mind separate or unified? How can we prove the existence of the outside world? Though such questions are serious and important, they fail to ask about existence itself. Heidegger's ontology, however, is concerned with the most fundamental of all questions. His question, 'What is the meaning of Being?' is prior to all other questions, since Being is prior to everything. This is why he called his approach a **fundamental ontology**.

A crucial difference in Heidegger's approach is that, unlike earlier philosophers, he makes no attempt to isolate human beings from the world in which they live. Traditionally philosophers have distinguished the 'knower' from the world it knows – the world is 'out there' and the thinker's task is to deal with what is in the mind, in relation to what is outside it. We are regarded as independently existing *thinking things*, completely separate from the world – we are the subjects, and the world is our object. Heidegger repudiates this approach, pointing out that I cannot look at the world 'objectively' because the world is not, and cannot possibly be, 'outside' me, since I am – and always have been since birth – *in* the world existing as a *part of it*. I am inextricably linked to all other entities in *a world-wide* web of significance.

AN ARGUMENT AGAINST HEIDEGGER'S APPROACH

One could argue that Being is not a thing, or entity. If it is not an entity, it does not exist; and if it does not exist, it cannot be known; if it cannot be known, any inquiry about its meaning is at best poetic and at worst meaningless.

Heidegger disagrees with this line of thinking for the following reasons:

* he disputes the assertion that Being does not exist.

* he is not striving to *know* Being, but to discover the *meaning* of Being as it expresses itself through mankind's way of Being, and humans definitely *do* exist.

Heidegger further justifies the relevance of questioning the meaning of Being, by pointing out the fact that most humans can, and actually do, wonder about the meaning of their existence. The occasional feeling of the utter *meaninglessness* of life, that almost everyone has experienced, is itself proof that the meaning of Being is under question. So Heidegger's inquiry into the meaning of Being is already relevant and active in us – we intuitively recognize it as a genuine question, even though we might regard it as unanswerable. So Heidegger's question is neither pointless, nor philosophically irrelevant.

HEIDEGGER'S RESPONSE TO NIHILISM
Nihilism is the denial that human existence has any significance at all. It asserts that there is no point in questioning existence in order to find principles for understanding it. In the very fact that Heidegger shows that it is worthwhile to ask about the meaning of Being, he is simultaneously revealing, not only that I exist, but that my life is *meaningful*. This is a clear rejection of the threat of nihilism, which Heidegger saw as the most destructive force on the planet.

HEIDEGGER'S VOCABULARY
One of the main objectives in Heidegger's philosophical style is to break the pattern of thinking that causes us to take Being for granted, and to make us question the meaning of Being – what it *means to be.* To achieve this aim he felt the need to construct a new way of thinking about Being that was distinct from any philosophical approach that had been used in the past. He was convinced that a specialized linguistic style and vocabulary was essential for this purpose. He considered language in general to be worn out from overuse, with its words gradually emptied of meaning and incapable of addressing existence adequately. His intention therefore was to develop a vocabulary and style of expression that would attune the language of his philosophy to the nature of Being.

'BEING' AND 'BEING'

To grasp Heidegger's thought, it is essential to begin with a clear understanding of two terms used throughout his writing – **being** (or **beings**) which is always written with a small 'b', and **Being**, which is always capitalized. The distinction between these two terms forms the foundation of Heidegger's entire philosophy. A being (or **entity**) refers to anything that has an existence of some sort – humans, animals, chairs, atoms, molecules, chemical processes; it is any event or thing in existence. In contrast to this, Heidegger uses the word 'Being' to refer to the existing 'isness' or **essence** of these entities – the primordial condition or fundamental **ground** that allows everything in the universe to come into existence. It is the shared factor of 'Being' that inhabits all entities, which makes our own existence inseparable from everything else – in this sense, all 'beings' truly are the same.

The original German term for 'Being' is *das Sein*. This noun is derived from *sein*, the infinitive 'to be'; in German it is quite usual to turn the infinitive form of a verb into a noun by capitalizing it. The literal translation therefore, of the noun *das Sein* is 'the to be'. So whenever the term Being with a capital 'B' is used in English books on Heidegger, the reader should bear in mind that the term 'Being' also includes the sense 'to be'. So a phrase such as 'the question of the meaning of Being,' also means 'to question what it means *to be*'. When reading Heidegger, 'Being' should never be thought of as an abstract noun or entity, nor regarded as referring to God, the universe or anything in it.

In spite of the difference in meaning of the two concepts 'Being' and 'being', each needs the other in order to make sense. Just as the notion of 'night' is nonsense without the existence of 'day', and vice versa, so *there can be no beings without Being and no Being without beings.*

To understand this relationship better, one could compare Being with *light* and beings with *vision*; light is the necessary pre-condition for seeing things – without light, human vision would be impossible. Similarly, Being is the necessary pre-condition for beings to exist.

Without Being – without the basic fact of existence in the first place – no human (or any other entity) could exist. Also, light itself cannot be seen – only the objects which are visible as a result of the light. Similarly Being cannot actually be seen – only the beings which exist as a consequence of Being. Heidegger then uses the adjective **ontological** to describe any information, statements, remarks or observations pertaining to Being. However, the major difficulty that is faced in ontology (the philosophy of Being) is that since Being is not an entity or 'thing', it does not have any measurable properties or characteristics. You can't see, hear or taste it, so the process of thinking about it and understanding it is very different from the straightforward observation, measurement and classification that is used to comprehend beings. Heidegger calls this dissimilarity between Being and beings an **ontological difference**. Heidegger also makes the seemingly paradoxical statement that Being is *nearest* to man, because it is the essence or 'isness' of his existence, and yet simultaneously it is *furthest* from him, because it is not an *entity* to which he can relate directly.

OURSELVES AS THE INITIAL SUBJECT-MATTER OF THE ENQUIRY

Since Being is invisible – hidden in the beings or things that it brings into existence – it cannot reveal itself outside of the beings it inhabits. *So Heidegger approaches the question of Being by investigating the Being of beings.* He believes that when any animate or inanimate entity is penetrated deeply by ontological thought, it has the potential to become what he calls a **clearing** (or instrument), through which Being reveals itself. To further illustrate the distinction between *ontic* and *ontological* investigation, we can look at how each would approach the examination of a piece of rock. An 'ontic' science, such as geology, will study the material composition and history of the rock, whereas **ontology** will attempt to 'think the Being of the rock'; it will try to understand that which gives it existence and how this manifests itself in the rock. In other words, ontology tries to experience and understand Being by immersing itself in the full 'thereness' or 'Beingness' of an entity. When this ontological thought achieves the required penetrative intensity, the being or entity then becomes a *clearing* or open space in which the true nature of Being will spontaneously reveal itself.

Although Being characterizes every entity whatsoever, Heidegger concluded that we should begin by first investigating our own way of Being – the way in which Being expresses itself through *us*.

Heidegger chooses us as the logical starting point for his inquiry, because he observed that we have a very unique and privileged relationship to Being – of all entities in existence, organic and inorganic, only humans can question, and seek to understand Being. We alone ask, 'What is Being?' Also, the very fact we raise the question in the first place clearly implies that we uniquely have some type of prior understanding of Being – however clouded it may be. For in order to ask *any* question, one needs some sort of understanding of the subject matter of the enquiry as well as a rough idea of where the answer might be found.

Heidegger describes our prior comprehension of Being as a *vague, average understanding of Being*. Even human beings who have never questioned the meaning of existence possess at least a rudimentary understanding of Being. Living in the world requires us to interact with all sorts of entities in our environment, which requires some level of understanding of our own Being as well as the Being of the entities which constitute our particular world. So in this sense, we also function as a unifying link between the entities existing in our world. Consequently, by choosing us as the starting point for his investigation of Being, Heidegger is not excluding other beings, for any investigation of our Being will automatically and necessarily include an investigation of the world of entities we inhabit.

Furthermore, unlike other entities that are encapsulated exclusively in a present moment and position, we are deeply rooted in a past heritage whilst simultaneously occupying the present and projecting forwards towards future possibilities, and we define who we are in terms of all this. So our Being is very much an issue for us. In contrast to this other forms of life – animals and plants for instance – are what they are. They are not required to determine their own existence or sense of identity.

TIME AS THE HORIZON OF BEING

To develop a deeper understanding of Being, Heidegger realized that we need to place it in an appropriate context. Heidegger calls this context the *horizon*. In the case of Being, Heidegger felt that *time* was the appropriate context. He therefore proposed that Being – the sense of what it means *to be* – could only be explored and understood *in relation to, or in terms of time.*

In his discussion of time, the question Heidegger asks himself is: 'What does it mean *to be* in time?' rather than: 'What *is* time?' If we believe, as some people claim, that the past is no more and therefore irrelevant to my 'here and now,' then the promise I made yesterday would not be meaningful or matter, because 'yesterday is no more'. We know instantly, however, that this is not the case. Nor is it relevant to argue that it is only *memory* which is important here, for memory is simply the means of *transporting* the past into the present. It seems intuitively impossible for me to reflect on what, or who, I am at this moment without taking into account what I have done in the past and my direction in life – which lies in the future. Though these observations may seem obvious, they expose a crucial point made by Heidegger – *the past, present and the future are an inextricable and significant part of our way of Being.*

Heidegger concludes that this present moment is meaningful to me, only in terms of my awareness of what I am actually doing right now. According to Heidegger, my *past* is also alive in the present, in the sense that it is responsible for my present circumstances. Furthermore, the past combines with my present situation and actions to create *and* limit my future possibilities. My future also exists in the present via my future choices, which in turn influence my present actions. Heidegger claims that the future is the most important dimension of my **temporality** because the choices I make for my future determine who I am now and, paradoxically, the future can also be the *source* of my past. For instance, a person from a very underprivileged background who becomes a successful businessman will interpret their past as a life of deprivation from which they have emerged. But to a novelist, this same past might be interpreted as a rich source of writing material. Furthermore, although the events of my past obviously cannot be *altered*, what my past *means* to me – how I experience and interpret it now – is completely determined by the conception I have of myself in terms of my future possibilities.

Heidegger's analysis leads him to the conclusion that 'Temporality makes up the primordial meaning of **Dasein's** (human beings) Being.' So in saying we are temporal, it is clear that Heidegger is not emphasizing the obvious fact that we are going to die, or that we have a sense of time, but rather that our way of Being simultaneously spans the three dimensions of time. The past, the present and the future exist in every moment of our existence and constitute who we are and also our current activities.

Since we live in a three-dimensional time zone, and *not* in quantifiable, geometric, linear time, this suggests that *time* itself is *also* three-dimensional – the past, present, and future are unified and indivisible. So, according to Heidegger, who we *are*, our *way of Being*, and the *significance* our existence has for us, can only be understood within the context of the totality of the unfolding process of our life, in terms of where we are coming from, and where we are going.

BEING AND TIME

So what actually is Heidegger's approach to answering the question of Being? In his great work *Being and Time*, which was published in 1927, he tried his utmost to answer the question, but he did not succeed, and the book was left unfinished. Later he claimed that Being is a continually evolving phenomenon that is 'intrinsically mysterious and self-concealing'. He concluded that the inherent limitations of human speech prevent us from intelligibly explaining the 'isness' or meaning of Being. Consequently we can only speak of it tautologically: 'Being is Being.' His dissatisfaction with the limitations of language is visible in one of his essays on Being '*Zur Seinesfrage*' in which he frequently crosses out the written word *Sein* (Being). Though obliged to use words when writing or speaking about Being, Heidegger is emphasizing here that one must not confuse these verbal representations of Being with the actual state of Being. The word 'Being' is not that to which it refers, as what it refers to is in a 'wordless' dimension. This is why Heidegger crosses the word out, to emphasize the absence of any sense of 'word-ness' in the state of Being.

Heidegger did acknowledge that such a thing as truth exists, and he viewed some interpretations of it, including his own, as better than others. He stated however his opinion that there is no final explanation – perceptions of truth are only relevant to the time and situation in which they arise. He was very much against the idea that there existed ultimate, universal truths that are independent of time and place. In reference to this Heidegger claimed 'I have no philosophy', because for him philosophy was not something one has – like a theory or set of principles – but the untiring passionate commitment to a question. He strongly believed that the primary objective in his work was not to provide answers to the question of Being, but to stimulate in us a keen awareness of the question. This can potentially make us receptive to experiencing the full force of its incredible mystery. Heidegger is not noted for offering convincing, reliable answers, but for his ceaseless questioning.

THE NOTHING
In 1929, he began a new angle of attack with regard to his search for the meaning of Being. On the occasion of his inauguration as professor at Freiburg, Heidegger delivered one of his most famous lectures: 'What

is Metaphysics?'. The final questions Heidegger asks in this lecture are 'Why is there something (beings), rather than Nothing? (Nothingness)' and 'What is the Nothing?'

From the point of view of logic, 'What is the Nothing?' makes sense only if it is considered to be a question about how the grammatical process of negation works. But, according to Heidegger, 'the Nothing' (or Nothingness) that he is talking about does not refer to the negation *not anything*; it is not the *negation* of Being. The root meaning of the word Nothingness supports this view: *No-thing-ness* does indeed suggest a 'presentness' or 'thereness' (which is not defined or limited by any particular existence or object). The Nothingness he is talking about here, far from being 'nothing at all' is regarded by Heidegger as a dynamic, creative force.

Heidegger claims that the 'Nothing' is constantly in the background of our existence. The state of deep **anxiety** (*Angst*) and despair, which sometimes arises in people for no apparent reason, is often caused by a sudden perception of the Nothing (that may or may not have occurred at a conscious level of awareness). This creates a sense of emptiness and insignificance. All beings appear to be threatened by the Nothing, which makes everything seem *non-sense*. Heidegger believes however that during moments of deep anxiety we can also sometimes become acutely aware of the Nothing in such a way that it opens our understanding to the true nature of Being.

He asserts that Being is finite, and is surrounded by the Nothing. He considered Being and the Nothing to be mutually dependent and indivisible, like two sides of a coin. This close connection between Being and Nothing is also evidenced by the fact that they share an important intrinsic attribute. Being (like Nothing) is not a thing – if it were, it would instead be a being (rather than Being) – so in this sense one can conclude that Being is *no-thing*. Humans participate in both Being, by existing, and the Nothing, by ceasing to exist. Only the two possibilities of Being and Nothing are constant. Heidegger felt that the world we live in, and the entities it contains, can only be understood in the light of this existence and non-existence of Being and Nothing.

Heidegger regards the Nothing as the creative womb from which Being emerges. Just as great works of art often emerge from artists who have been through great suffering, the Nothing has the potential to expand our consciousness into an illuminated perception of existence. Acknowledging the Nothing can stimulate an intense awareness of the dramatic contrast between beings and the Nothing. The background threat, anxiety or sense of the insignificance of everything, cleanses our vision and allows us to see that there *is* a great difference between something (beings) and Nothing. An awareness of the Nothing can wake us out of our habitual manner of viewing life so that we find new meaning in existence and in the beings which inhabit it. Being is only meaningful because it lives constantly in the shadow of the seeming meaninglessness of the Nothing. In Heidegger's words: 'Without the original revelation of the Nothing, no selfhood and no freedom.' Awareness of this Nothingness restores in *Dasein* (human beings) the feeling of primal astonishment in the face of Being, and simultaneously generates an awareness of the fact that at the heart of Being is generative Nothingness.

WHY IS THERE SOMETHING RATHER THAN NOTHING?

Heidegger's comments about the potentially creative force of the Nothing still shed no light on his main query, 'Why is there something rather than Nothing?' This question seems to reach beyond the power of human reason – no scientific investigation or theology is capable of providing the answer. The Big Bang theory, if it is correct, does not answer why there *was* a Big Bang in the first place, rather than Nothing. One may believe God made the Big Bang, but then why is there a God? Whatever we propose as the cause of everything, is itself something that has an existence that requires explanation. It seems that the question Heidegger poses is unanswerable. Many philosophers argue that this implies that the question is meaningless – they claim convincingly that the word 'Nothing' which Heidegger uses means exactly that – nothing at all. And yet no matter how plausible any such arguments may be, the question still seems relevant to us at some level of our awareness. The cosmologist Stephen Hawking clearly affirms the significance of Heidegger's question when he writes, 'once science has described how everything works, we will still want to ask: What is it that breathes fire into the equations and makes a universe for them to describe … Why does the universe go to all the bother of existing?'

THE SIGNIFICANCE OF UNANSWERABLE QUESTIONS

So what is it that makes the question of the meaning of Being so important to Heidegger – if it cannot actually be answered, then how can it possibly have any meaning at all?

It is precisely the non-answerable nature of this question that Heidegger finds so intriguing and meaningful. He distinguishes between two sorts of questions. The first type (ontic questions), such as 'How far away is the moon from the earth?', have terminal answers. Heidegger regards these as trivial, since the answer settles the question and renders it inert – there is nothing further to be gained from asking it again. The second type (ontological questions) which he views as 'worthy of questioning', are unanswerable and therefore inexhaustible. Heidegger regarded the action of focusing on 'worthy questions' as the path to man's 'homecoming to the House of Being'. For him, the most worthy of such questions is the question of Being. Heidegger believed strongly that only when humans are able to feel a sense of harmony with the paradoxical nature of this question, would they have found their way home.

He often reiterated that one should avoid all attempts to subject Being to logical analysis and formal definition – 'when we seek to articulate Being, it is always as though we are reaching into the void'. Instead he emphasized that the only legitimate tactic for investigating Being was questioning. A mind fully absorbed in the activity of intense authentic questioning, gradually enters into a state of deep connection or oneness with that which is being questioned. Just as a guitar string will 'sympathetically resonate' with a string of the same pitch that is vibrating on a guitar nearby, perhaps the process of Heidegger's questioning allows the Being of the questioner to sympathetically resonate with the awesome and amazing phenomenon of Universal Being.

So it would seem reasonable to conclude that Heidegger's 'Why is there something rather than nothing?' is not actually a question that is asking for an answer, but rather an expression of sheer astonishment and wonder over the fact of existence. Heidegger claimed that, in the mood of astonishment, the questioner is most receptive to hearing the 'voice of Being' – to becoming closely attuned to and aware of the nature of Being. As the poet Coleridge put it, 'in Wonder all Philosophy began'.

We have become so accustomed to life, that in our normal state of consciousness we take everything for granted. But there are occasions when we may suddenly become aware of the miracle of existence. At such times questions like 'Why is there something, rather than nothing?' may be as close as we can come to expressing the thoughts and feelings that accompany our profound realization. When Heidegger asks this question, he is revealing and expressing his awareness of the marvellous mystery of Being and he encourages us to ask the same question, so that we may experience this realization for ourselves.

Heidegger's great passion was asking questions, not providing answers. The purpose of his inquiry was to reinstill the mystery of life that has been receding into oblivion through the passage of time. Even if one ultimately disagrees with every claim found in Heidegger's writings, they are still worth reading, because the primary task of a philosopher is to alert us to what is worthy of questioning. There is no doubt that this has been accomplished with regard to the question of the meaning of Being.

3 The Central Concepts of *Being and Time*

In *Being and Time*, Heidegger's investigation of the meaning of Being is carried out via an analysis of human existence. Heidegger does not separate the study of Being from the study of humanity because he sees no difference – he asserts that we cannot have the one without the other, so *Being and Time* is simultaneously an analysis of *our* way of Being *and* an inquiry into the *meaning* of Being. The study has a 'spiral' structure, in the sense that Heidegger continually reinterprets the facets of our existence on increasingly deeper levels that provide a deeper understanding of our own Being – the truth of who we are – thus getting closer to an understanding of the meaning of Being as a whole.

DASEIN – OURSELVES AS THE STARTING POINT

This journey begins with Heidegger's most prominent new term – *Dasein*. In English books on his work, this word is usually left untranslated. Prior to Heidegger, in the eighteenth century, philosophers such as Kant and Husserl began using this pure German construction, which means 'existence', instead of the previously used Latin-derivative **existenz**. For these philosophers, the term could be used to refer to the existence of any entity – animate or inanimate. Heidegger's usage of the word however carries quite different connotations. He uses the term *Dasein* to refer exclusively to *us* and our *way of Being*, in place of the standard German terminology for man or human being. The word has no plural so it can refer to a single human being as well as all human beings.

Heidegger chose to use this innovative expression, *Dasein*, for several reasons. To begin with, he felt that the words we use no longer adequately express their original sense – they have become 'worn out' from over-use, so we miss their deeper significance. In using *Dasein*, however, he awakens our awareness and inspires us to look at ourselves with fresh eyes. He hoped this would encourage us to think about who we are in a revolutionary manner – uninfluenced by the traditional opinions of religion, philosophy, psychology and anthropology. Heidegger specifically selected the term *Dasein* because he felt that it best encapsulated, emphasized and expressed the fact that our *way of Being*, or existing, is qualitatively very different from all other entities, and it is this which makes humans unique.

Our distinct and special way of Being is reflected in the linguistic structure of the term *Dasein*. To begin with, this noun is also the infinitive form of a verb (to exist), which suggests one of the distinguishing features Heidegger attributes to humanity, namely that we are more like an *activity* or *process* than any sort of *thing*. However, the characteristic in our way of Being which most differentiates us from other beings, is reflected in Heidegger's emphasis of the root meaning of the word *Dasein*, which is 'there being', or 'being there' from *da* (there) and *Sein* (being). His use of 'there' in this context refers to the world and the unique way we are able to inhabit it, with a capacity for understanding existence that does not exist in any other entities.

There is one final important meaning contained in the term *Dasein* that Heidegger only stresses in his later years. He claims that the 'there' of 'Being there' is in fact *us*, and that we are *there* on behalf of Being – that we are in a sense the 'guardians of Being'. Heidegger claims that we are the 'clearing' or 'open space' in which Being is able to express itself. Without *Dasein*, the world as we know it would cease to exist – other entities would continue to exist, but there would be no one to relate to them as entities, so their *Being* would have no meaning at all and, in a sense, would therefore not exist.

THE *A PRIORI* STRUCTURE OF *DASEIN*

At the root of Heidegger's entire enterprise in *Being in Time* is his claim that *Dasein* has an **a priori** awareness of its own existence, in other words, we possess a rudimentary comprehension of our existence, prior to any life experience, that allows us to make sense of the world we live in. Heidegger explains this understanding in terms of various *a priori* **existentials**. Each existential refers to a specific *a priori* mode of *Dasein*'s Being and understanding. Heidegger analyses all these existentials, which together constitute *Dasein*'s complete *a priori* way of understanding and Being in the world, and this forms the basis of *Dasein*'s capacity to question and investigate the meaning of Being.

THE WORLD

Heidegger's conception of *Dasein* describes its Being as a 'being-there' in which 'there' refers to the **world**. Heidegger's usage of 'world' in this sense refers to the entire circumstances or context that influence a particular *Dasein*'s total existence. This includes its country of residence, the particular culture and social environment, education, family, friends, career and pastimes etc. For instance, a particular lawyer's 'world' would consist of the sum total of his own life situation – all of his interests and activities as a lawyer, a father, an Englishman and so on. Another *Dasein*, for example, might inhabit primarily a business world or alternatively, a sporting world, academic world or entertainment world.

The world in which a particular *Dasein* is involved will determine his reaction to life events. For instance, a surgeon who has nothing to do with the business world may not be even slightly upset by a stock market crash, whereas a *Dasein* who is a stockbroker is likely to be devastated. So any particular *Dasein* will be defined by involvement in a particular world or worlds. Western philosophers have traditionally tried to observe 'objectively' and understand humanity by 'lifting' people out of their *world* in order to isolate an independent 'essence' or 'pure consciousness'. Heidegger considers this approach as completely erroneous, futile and misleading, for he considers *Dasein* as being inextricably enmeshed or rooted *in the world*. To stress this point Heidegger often hyphenates *Dasein* so that the literal translation of *Da-sein* as 'there-being', in which 'there' refers to the world, now becomes 'world-being'.

DASEIN'S BEING-IN-THE-WORLD

The first *a priori existential* that Heidegger describes therefore, is *Dasein*'s **Being-in-the-world**. What Heidegger means by 'Being-in' is our *a priori* capacity to understand, relate to, care about and concern ourselves with the things in the world around us. His use of hyphens emphasizes his view of the world and *Dasein* as an indivisible unity. *Dasein* however, blinded by the apparent banality of the world, tends to be unaware of the crucial significance of being-in-the-world. But in the same way that a tree cannot be truly appreciated or understood when it has been uprooted and removed from its place of growth, so Heidegger emphatically asserts that *Dasein* cannot possibly be comprehended in isolation from the world it inhabits. *Dasein* is fused with the world – it is not possible to separate *Dasein* from the world as it is *Dasein*'s most 'vital organ' – the fundamental source of *Dasein*'s existence.

DASEIN'S ORDINARY, EVERYDAY EXISTENCE

Although there may be vast differences between the various worlds a *Dasein* might inhabit, there is a basic underlying *infrastructure,* or Being, that they all share – Heidegger calls this the **worldhood** of the world. This term is used to refer to the totality of all our practical functional relationships with everything in our world. Heidegger believes that to understand the infrastructure of *worldhood*, and thus better understand ourselves, we need analyse our way of living in the ordinary, everyday reality of the immediate world around us. Heidegger describes how the world is experienced and made meaningful to us through our practical involvement or relations to the things (entities) around us, which we employ for a useful purpose to accomplish our goals. He emphasizes that the practical world is primordial, as it is the one we inhabit prior to any form of philosophizing or scientific investigation, and it is where we spend the majority of our time. It is only when we use something that we can really understand it. 'Detached' or 'objective' thinking about things is derived from the practical world, not vice versa, and this detachment from entities artificially disables our contact with the practical world so we lose our deep sense of the nature of things. According to Heidegger, we possess an *a priori* understanding of our being-in-the-world that allows us a prior sense of the practical potential of the things in our environment. Our awareness of the world and its entities is then *increased* via our practical involvement in, or relationship with, all the entities around us. Heidegger uses the term **circumspection** to describe the kind of involved (rather than detached or objective) 'looking around' that has a practical motive – which takes place in, and which is guided by the demands of practical interests or activities. Circumspection recognizes how **ready-to-hand** entities relate to one another.

READY-TO-HAND AND PRESENT-AT-HAND

Heidegger's analysis reveals that the entities we encounter in everyday life do not all have the same way of Being – to bring attention to this important fact he describes their Being as either **ready-to-hand** or **present-at-hand**, terms that are applicable only in reference to non-human entities. It is the way we relate to a particular entity that determines which classification is applicable. If something is regarded by *Dasein* as having a useful function for human purposes, then for this *Dasein* the entity is *ready-to-hand*, or **equipment** – a Heideggerian abbreviation meaning the same thing. Relating to entities as ready-to-hand is *Dasein*'s fundamental way of Being-in-the-world – Heidegger calls these relations of **concern**.

In contrast to this, *present-at-hand* is Heidegger's description of the Being of entities for which we have no use or interest, or alternatively their significance to us may be merely one of detached, objective interest in, or observation of, their physical properties. The same object can also sometimes be present-at-hand, and at other times ready-to-hand, depending upon the way one relates to it. Natural entities, such as rocks, that have a completely neutral resting state, are generally experienced as present-at-hand – but for a stonemason who makes use of them, they are quite definitely ready-to-hand.

Manufactured artefacts or raw materials that serve human purposes in some way are usually experienced as ready-to-hand, but a piece of equipment (ready-to-hand entity) that is broken, rendered useless, or in the hands of someone who does not know what it is for, is quite definitely experienced as present-at-hand.

To take an example, a screwdriver to a car mechanic who is occupied repairing a car, is without doubt experienced as ready-to-hand, but for a rainforest tribesman the same screwdriver will invariably be seen as being present-at-hand. If however the screwdriver is broken, and therefore useless, the mechanic will then experience it as **unready-to-hand** – Heidegger's term for the present-at-hand condition of equipment that is broken or rendered unusable. Similarly, in the case of a carpenter working on wood with a hammer and nails, all three items will be experienced as ready-to-hand. If however he runs out of nails, or misplaces his hammer and consequently can no longer use the remaining tools and materials, he will now regard them as present-at-hand (unready-to-hand). Conversely, someone might come across an apparently neutral, useless object, which later turns out to be useful to them. Though initially perceiving the thing as present-at-hand, they will now experience it as ready-to-hand.

HEIDEGGER'S 'EQUIPMENT TOTALITY'

When *Dasein* relates to a ready-to-hand item it understands the item as fundamentally existing within a *network* of other entities. This network reveals where things belong and how they fit into our lives. Our understanding of this is *a priori* and generally subliminal (though, in a very conscious *Dasein*, this awareness may be frequent). An example of this *entity network* is evident in the simple act of writing: I pick up a pen in order to write a letter. The paper I use exists in order to be written on, the envelope 'in order to' contain the letter, the stamp to pay for it, the post box to receive it in order for the postman to deliver it. This 'in order to' indicates the chain of connection between entities in *Dasein*'s environment. Thus 'one tool is ontologically impossible'; a tool is always part of an implicit network of interreferential equipment in *Dasein*'s place of work. A hammer exists within the network of other related tools, raw materials, the job it is used for, its end result or product etc. This collection of instruments and materials related to a ready-to-hand item Heidegger calls **equipment totality**. The system of ongoing purposes and projects that describe the relations between our activities and goals, he refers to as 'towards which', 'in order to' and 'for the sake of'. We can see from the above example how the everyday world is characterized by a large network of practical relations between all the things and humans in our environment that are in any way, however remote or indirectly, related to *Dasein*'s purposes or goals.

We do not typically pay much attention to the things we use, nor their 'referential totality' (their existence in a network). Practical things around us serve their instrumental function invisibly, as our mind is on our work, not on the equipment that helps us to acccomplish it. According to Heidegger, this generally defines our relationship with the tools of our practical activities. However, when something we use malfunctions, breaks down or goes missing we suddenly become aware of the network of relations in which its functioning was embedded. For instance when a doorknob comes off in my hand, I might suddenly notice how it belongs to the latch of the door leading to the hallway that I need to walk down, to get into my office to collect a book for a lecture – the world of practical activity is thus very clearly revealed to me. So *Dasein*'s involvement with ready-to-hand equipment lights up the surrounding character of the *worldhood* of our world as being a unified web of significance – which is often of *practical* significance. In contrast, the detached 'objective' present-at-hand experience of things is relevant and essential in areas such as science where theories are a neccessity, but it is only a very specialized, highly restricted way of seeing things that is fundamentally derived from our experience of Being-in-the-world.

Heidegger emphasizes that when we view life principally as a collection of independently existing animate and inanimate entities, or if we treat things generally as *present-at-hand*, we are limiting ourselves to a very narrowed perception of Being. We are disregarding our fundamental unity with the world, the interconnectedness of everything around us and our practical and personal concerns which constitute our primary way of Being in the world. This attitude allows humans to be treated as ciphers in statistics as though they are mere present-at-hand 'scientific objects' or, alternatively, as ready-to-hand 'tools' for business or political purposes.

SPACE AND TIME

Heidegger also pays close attention to the role that space and time play with regards to our experience of the significance of the entities around us. He is not interested in the formally measured, objective scientific sense of space, but rather with our *spatial experience* of the *significance* of things which is influenced by our concern for what is experienced and the mood we are in. This concept of space leads to some strange, but very normal phenomena. For example, how *near* something is to us is measured and is significant to us primarily in terms of its *availability for use.* And a caller on the telephone may be perceived as nearer than someone in the same room if our concern and attention are with the caller and not the person with us in the room. So practical concern, understanding and states of mind can make space stretch or contract. In addition, *Dasein* often experiences the objects it uses in its environment as significant in terms of their existence in all three dimensions of time – the past, the possible futures and the present moment. For example, the existence of a bicycle I ride may be significant to me in terms of its past, seen in paintwork scratches from minor accidents. It also signifies all the possible rides I will have on it in the future, and as I am riding it I feel the pleasure of freedom in the present moment.

BEING-WITH-OTHERS

Up until this point, Heidegger has described *Dasein*'s existence in the everyday world as characterized by a purposeful use of things in the environment, which exist in an extended network that defines their connection with one another and their role in our lives.

He now asks '*who* it is that *Dasein* is in its everydayness'. He is not interested in answering this question via self-conscious introspection, which invariably leads to conceptions of 'self' as some kind of independently existing or transcendental 'thing'. For Heidegger, *Dasein* is not any sort of 'thing', and introspection is not *Dasein*'s fundamental or normal way of Being – so the conclusions I reach via this approach, usually lead to false assumptions about who I normally am.

Heidegger therefore suggests that I should investigate who I was *before* I began to reflect, whilst I was still absorbed with my life in the everyday world. According to Heidegger this leads to the realization that in my Being-in-the-world I always, and essentially, experience things in relation to *other people*. As long as I exist, I am always with others in some way. All my material possessions depend on others, and virtually everything I do requires others – at work, during holidays, leisure activities and in medical matters. My world is essentially a public or social world. Even when there are no other people around – for example, on a deserted station platform, or when working in isolation – others are conspicuous by their absence, and they are *there* via the man-made things around me.

Heidegger calls this communal dimension of *Dasein*'s Being-in-the-world, **Being-with**, and he asserts that this is a fundamental feature of *Dasein*'s Being. He states 'the world of *Dasein* is a "with-world"'.

It is important to realize that Heidegger regards Being-with as an *a priori* existential which enables Dasein to relate to others. In other words, Being-with is the *a priori* dimension of the self, which provides us with the *potential* to understand and relate to others in all possible ways. So *Dasein* always has the capacity to relate to others, and that is why its Being is a *Being-with*. So even if I have been deprived of all human contact since earliest childhood, because I live on a deserted island with no man-made products, I would still be a Being-with, because it is my *a priori* inheritance from mankind. In Heidegger's words: 'Even *Dasein*'s being alone is being-with in the world.'

DASEIN'S THROWNNESS

We are 'thrown' into the world, according to Heidegger. The random forces of chance or destiny determine our country and place of birth, race, religion, culture and the family and environment surrounding us – our *world*. Aside from knowing the facts of our conception and birth, ultimately – from the larger more universal perspective – we have no idea whatsoever where we came from, or why we are here. We did not choose any of the aspects of our existence and yet they fundamentally influence our current situation and all our future possibilities for Being. Heidegger calls this event of being thrust into an involuntary existence our **thrownness**, and the 'burden' we carry as a result is termed our **facticity**. Our facticity is the sum total of our current situation, combined with what this enables us to become in terms of our own future *possibilities*.

Thrownness is a central feature of *Dasein*, and according to Heidegger, it is not an inert, completed fact that is over and done with, like the early history of one's family tree. The momentum of *Dasein*'s 'throw' never diminishes – *Dasein* remains permanently in the state of being thrown, and this influences and shapes his entire existence. I am *thrown* out of the past and into the present whilst *projecting* from within my thrownness towards the future. The term 'projection' refers to *Dasein*'s efforts to fulfil its own possibilities. I can never get *behind* or break free from my thrownness. To emphasize this Heidegger uses the peculiar double adverb that appears throughout *Being and Time* – *always already*. He points out I am always a *Being-already-in-the-world*. Our possibilities are determined by the chance event of our thrownness, which is responsible for where we always already are, and who we always already are.

In other words, my thrownness means that I have a *past* I always carry with me, that must serve as a foundation for my *present* existence and which defines and limits my *future* possibilities. My projections for the future are always *thrown* and even my creative achievements are *thrown*, because the choices I make, and all I create, must be made on the basis of what I already am at the moment, which is influenced by my past – the continuing momentum of my thrownness. So I can never create myself anew, as I have to work with what I *have been* and what I *am now*, in order to become what I want to be in the *future*. Consequently there is a continual struggle between the drive to actualize my potentials and the influences or restraints of my thrownness. The fact of my thrownness shows that, in the final analysis, I can never say I have really chosen my current situation because ultimately everything I am and do has been made possible by the 'already given' situation into which I was thrown.

INAUTHENTICITY: THE 'THEY–SELF'

Heidegger claims, that we live most of the time in a constant state of **inauthenticity**. The inauthentic mode of living is characterized by a lack of self-awareness that is rooted in our absorption in the ways of living that *others* provide us. As Heidegger says: 'The self of everyday *Dasein* is the *they-self*, which we distinguish from the *authentic Self*.' The **they-self** is Heidegger's term for the inauthentic mode of the self. He explains it by pointing out that *Dasein*'s primordial state of *Being-with* (the social context of its world) includes a fundamental feature called the *they*. This refers to the full range of social and cultural customs, expectations and interpretations of life, offered by the particular world that *Dasein* inhabits. As the *they-self*, Dasein adopts the 'way of the *they*'.

From birth, *Dasein* lives as the 'they-self', and so its understanding, behaviour, and basic mode of survival is shaped by the ready-made explanations, evaluations and standards of the 'they' of the particular society and period in time into which it is *thrown*. It makes *Dasein*'s existence meaningful and comprehensible. So our way of living and self-understanding is rooted in, and complies with, the anonymous public 'they' – we behave, speak, and value as 'one' speaks, behaves, and values. In the world of the 'they', there is a *levelling off* of distinctions and a *levelling down* of possibilities – at school, children who are 'different' are rejected until they learn to conform to the *they-world* of their peers.

The 'they' instills in us the sense we have of ourselves, and the world around us. It even subliminally influences the physical distance we maintain in social situations. When the space dictated by the 'they' of one culture, differs greatly from that of another culture, there is social incompatibility.

One can see the influence of the 'they' everywhere, even in a *Dasein*'s clothes and hairstyle. Each *Dasein* adopts an appearance that essentially conforms to the 'they' of their particular *world*. The businessman adopts a style in keeping with the 'business they', and *Dasein* in each of the uniformed services (police, military etc.) have a 'they' which determines *their* style.

Members of the rebellious world of counter-culture who think they are escaping the influence of the 'they', by 'doing their *own* thing', with their supposedly imaginative hairstyles, body-piercings, tatooing and 'cool' clothes, are deluding themselves. These types are merely conforming to the *they* of the counter-culture world. Indeed, the so-called 'non-conformist' is invariably a rigid conformist within his or her own subculture.

INAUTHENTICITY: FALLING

Inauthenticity is characterized by what Heidegger calls **fallenness**. He says: 'Fallenness into the world means an absorbtion in Being-with-one-another, in so far as the latter is guided by idle talk, curiosity, and ambiguity.' He asserts that in the state of *falling*, talk becomes inauthentic speech which is manifested in *idle chatter* in the form of gossip about trivia – restless, empty talk that echoes no real truth. The counterpart of this in writing is called *scribbling* – popular writing that is absorbing, distracting and 'disburdening' and typical of newspapers and popular fiction. The inauthentic attitude towards the world is characterized by *idle curiosity* and *indifference*. Genuine interest in things is replaced by superficial curiosity that lusts for novelty in the form of the most recent fashions and the latest news and varied entertainment – a shallow understanding of insignificant media topics that reflect the interests of the 'they'.

A common example of *falling* is finding ourselves in a store in front of a rack that is filled with attractive looking magazines and newspapers covering every possible subject. We pick up one publication after another speedily browsing through articles on health and fitness or celebrity gossip, the latest computer or hi-fi gear and numerous newspaper headlines to get up-to-date on the latest world events. Everything seems fascinating, and our attention becomes absorbed in one article after another – but only very superficially and briefly, before it is sidetracked to the next topic. Suddenly, as if coming out of a trance, we jolt back into our bodies and carry on with our lives again. But we are left with the uncomfortable feeling that what we indulged in was a complete waste of valuable time.

In fallenness one drifts along with the fads and trends of the crowd, caught up in the mindless busy-ness, and tranquilized by the secure feeling that everyone else is doing the same thing – things in general seem to have been worked out by us. Heidegger says that, in its fallenness, *Dasein* 'becomes blind to all its possibilities, and tranquilizes itself with that which is merely 'actual."' In its simplest form, *fallenness is the non-awareness of what it means to be.*

Heidegger asserts that fallenness is an automatic and direct consequence of our thrownness and thus a basic feature of the human predicament. *Dasein*, in its fallenness, spends most of the time absorbed by the practical matters of daily survival. It attends to its present concerns – busy at the word processor, or involved in business deals over the phone. Its 'authentic ability to be itself' is thus buried beneath its current preoccupations and shallow interests of its dead past and future desires. It pays no attention to its thrownness and therefore lacks an overall perspective of its life from birth to death. Consequently its self-concept is defined by its current situation in life rather than in terms of its future possibilities.

When we live inauthentically, our general way of living is based upon a *means-ends* perspective on life, in which all our actions are *in order to get something*. So we might swim fifty lengths per day in order to get healthy. We might live for weeks on a diet we dislike, in order to get thin. We might accept dinner invitations in order to make contacts. In addition, we constantly check our performance against public criteria, because we worry about what others think of us and fear that we will not meet the standards of success set by the 'they' of our particular 'world.' In this *means-ends* approach to life, our moment-by-moment existence becomes unimportant as we are like the proverbial donkey chasing the carrot at the end of the stick, unconcerned with the *quality* of the route we are taking.

Heidegger explains, however, that the inauthentic condition of *Dasein*'s Being serves a neccessary function in everyday life. The acceptance of our pre-established ways of existence allows us to interpret our daily circumstances and deal with our practical concerns. If everyone constantly challenged this 'given' basis for existence – our conventional ways of thinking and living – we would have no solid foundation for interpreting life around us and society would come to a halt. We would all find ourselves on the edge of what Heidegger describes as 'the abyss of meaninglessness'.

So when Heidegger uses the term 'inauthenticity', he is definitely *not* suggesting that it is less real than authenticity. He emphasizes that *Dasein*'s inauthentic existence characterized by fallenness and the they-self has nothing to do with *wrong* choices or moral failings, but is part of the structure of normal everyday existence in the world. He also asserts that the process of becoming deeply aware of our *inauthentic* modes of Being (in the experience of profound *anxiety*) highlights the structure of *authenticity*.

MOODS

Moods are a primordial part of *Dasein*'s essential character and way of Being. *Dasein* is never *moodless* – it is always in one mood or another. Even apparently moodless states such as indifference are themselves a type of mood. And the dispassionate activity of 'objective' scientific investigation is also characterized by a mood – perhaps one of fascination or wonder. Similarly the condition of seemingly 'moodless', detached, meditative contemplation or observation, in which everything is 'flattened out' to a uniform realm of purposeless objects, is also a type of mood – according to Heidegger, a '*tranquil* dwelling on'.

So we are always in some kind of mood, and to be in a particular mood is to view the totality of our existence in a particular way, which in turn influences our feelings and behaviour in the world. In the mood of deep boredom all things are revealed to us as dull, inspiration vanishes and we usually become inactive.

The intense mood of anxiety fills us with a sense of dread so that existence appears senseless – all ambition seems futile and our achievements shrink into insignificance as we sense, in our deepest Being, the inevitability of our own death. In contrast, the mood of love can render life full of significance, beauty and magic and we feel motivated. Heidegger however focuses his discussion primarily on those moods in which 'the burdensome character of *Dasein*' is revealed – the moods in which we realize that the essence of who we are is beyond our control.

He describes our most common everyday mood as 'the pallid, evenly balanced lack of mood' which contains traces of irritation and boredom. Everyday activity is often an escape from that mood – we refuse to look at the 'burdensome character of *Dasein*' which the mood potentially reveals to us – for as Heidegger explains, '*Dasein* for the most part evades the Being which is disclosed in the mood'. Ordinary everyday moods however, attune us to everyday requirements, whereas moods like intense anxiety or deep boredom, that reveal fundamental truths of existence, reveal nothing of the practical nature of things or current threats in the surrounding environment.

So to be in a mood is to be 'tuned into' life in a certain way, and this influences the nature of our understanding at any given moment. Sometimes, however, our mood may be completely inappropriate for the situation, and our perception of things will be so restricted that we may completely miss what is going on around us. For instance, if my general mood is exceptionally elated I might not notice the angry vibrations in a crowded room, whereas someone else in an irritable mood, who accurately tunes in and understands what is going on, might find the atmosphere intolerable.

Dasein's moods arise out of our *past* and thus disclose our *thrownness*. This truth is reflected in everyday statements such as 'I got up on the wrong side of bed this morning', which refers to the past – to the fact that I find I have been *thrown* into the world in a particular way that has put me in an *overall* bad *mood*. My getting up on the wrong side of bed is not the *dead* past, for it lives on with me as a burden in my present situation. Heidegger asserts that intense moods such as anxiety and deep existential boredom can reveal with intensity the bare nature of existence as it is, without the 'trappings' of job, house or personal social life. They are therefore a vital source of insight into the nature of our Being-in-the-world. Such moods reveal the uncontrollable fact of our thrownness – that our existence is largely determined by conditions and circumstances of the past that influence our present and determine our choices for the future. We discover that our existence truly matters and that our current way of living is largely inauthentic. In contrast to this, emotions such as fear, characterized by a 'fight or flight' response to an avoidable threat, conceal our potential for contacting authentic self. Similarly, ordinary *everyday moods* rarely provide any fundamental insight, as they usually entail an avoidance of authentic perception.

Heidegger emphasizes several important differences between moods and emotions. Since *moods* are involved with and reveal 'Being-in-the-world as a whole' he regards them as existentially far more important than *emotions* which only disclose *specific* things. For instance, fear reveals something particular, such as a guard dog, as a potential threat. I am bored *with a book,* angry with *someone* or about *something* or over a *certain* situation. But in contrast to this, I can also be in a generally angry *mood* without being angry about anything in particular (though whilst in this state it is likely that I will also become *emotionally* angry). Also, emotions are 'triggered' by something that happens, whereas, though it is possible to drive oneself *into* a mood, the essential characteristic of moods is that they come and go as they please, sometimes creeping up on us slowly and unobtrusively and sometimes striking like lightning, without warning. Heidegger also points out that *emotions* are founded upon *moods,* which are a primordial mode of *Dasein*'s way of Being.

Moods differ from emotions in another important way. I can sometimes control emotions, for instance if fear arises in me as I step into a bar that has a threatening atmosphere, I can escape it by leaving immediately. In contrast to this, the mood of dread which results from the awareness of the inevitability of my own death, or alternatively, the profound boredom that is not caused by any specific thing that I can avoid, are conditions *not* under my control. It is however possible to invoke moods. Some music has the power to produce in the listener intense moods of sadness, elation or even dread. The music accompanying films takes advantage of this to disclose the underlying *mood* of the storyline – excitement, contentment or ordinary average everydayness.

Heidegger asserts that there is a basic philosophical mood, which is a prerequisite for true understanding. In the absence of this mood, ideas that previously have been deeply grasped are now experienced as a tiresome jumble of 'word husks' and 'forced' concepts.

UNDERSTANDING

Heidegger says that all **understanding** is circular, in the sense that 'any interpretation which is to contribute understanding must already have understood what is to be interpreted'. In other words, all interpretations are based on a prior *context of intelligibility*.

So, in the philosophical realm as well as in the everyday world, *Dasein* always possesses a preliminary, rudimentary understanding of anything that it asks about or interprets. This prior understanding, inspires, guides and enables *Dasein* to question existence and make interpretations of the world.

Dasein possesses a prior understanding of its everyday world, the things in it and how it fits into this world – this includes an innate capacity to recognize tools or equipment for what they are. This is a part of *Dasein*'s Being-in-the-world. According to Heidegger, however, the chief characteristic of understanding is to *project* or *see* things in terms of their future *possibilities*. To understand myself and thus find meaning in myself, is to be aware of my *own* possibilities and to realize that I not only *have* possibilities; I *am* my possibilities. In being aware of my own possibilities I realize I have a choice between authentic choices, in which my own Being is significant, and inauthentic choices, in which the Being of the *they-self* is significant. *Dasein*'s authentic understanding essentially consists of the awareness of its own range of available possibilities, which are the already 'given' concrete possibilities of the worldly situation into which it has been *thrown*. So this understanding involves a holistic projection of a context in which particular possibilities become intelligible. In this light, Heidegger's statement 'Become what you are' makes good sense. This may seem paradoxical, as logic suggests that one can only *become* what one is *not yet*. What Heidegger means by this, is that what we *are* is the concrete *given* possibilities of our *thrownness*, and these possibilities, which constitute what we always *already* are, and who we always *already* are, are what we should develop and thus *become*. To become what one is, however, requires interpretation. Interpretation is the concrete working-through of the possibilities projected by understanding.

INTERPRETATION

In **interpretation**, we immediately see things *as* something. So when we see a motorcycle, we do not see a shape and some colours and hear some noises, and then infer that we are seeing a motorcycle. Instead, we first see a motorcycle, and only secondarily we may possibly choose to abstract its properties.

When we understand the purpose or usability of an item, we are interpreting or explaining its **as-structure**, which means that we are seeing its practical significance in terms of the possibilities it opens up for us – Heidegger called this an interpretation of the 'in order to' function. The kettle exists *in order to* boil water; the heater exists *in order to* keep me warm. This interpretation of the practical purpose of things, and their relation to other items in the environment, is the primary way we understand our daily reality. In fact it is unnatural and difficult to see something without noticing what it is and what it is for.

The interpretation of this *as-structure* is based upon our primordial *ready-to-hand* relationship with our everyday environment, where we experience entities as being in a contextual web of significant relations or involvements with other entities. A prior awareness of something's place within this web is a prequisite to interpreting its *as-structure*. This background, 'global' understanding is what Heidegger calls the **fore-structure** of understanding. Heidegger divides this fore-structure into three separate parts, though all are simultaneously active during any given act of interpretation. *Fore-having* is the general understanding of the entity to be interpreted and of the complete context in which it is involved. The fore-having of a mechanic will be his global understanding of everything in his workshop, whereas a psychologist would have a broad understanding of human nature. *Fore-sight* sets its sights on what is to be interpreted (or a specific feature of it). The mechanic will focus his attention on an engine, or a specific mechanical fault in it, whereas the psychologist might construct a personality profile of an individual or focus on one specific behavioural dysfunction. *Fore-conception* refers to the fact that it is only possible to interpret things in terms of the concepts of which one is aware. Though I may be able to see something as a tool, I will not be able to see it as a 'monkey wrench' if I lack the concept of a 'monkey wrench'. This fore-structure is in play during interpretations at every level of sophistication.

MEANING

Meaning is what one arrives at when understanding becomes aware of the *as-structure* of entities. To comprehend the meaning of something, therefore, is to understand its function whilst simultaneously seeing its network of significant purposive relationships with other entities. It is because *Dasein* has a primordial sense of its own existence, as part of a network of meaningful relationships to other entities, that it understands its Being and its own possibilities in relation to its Being-in-the-world as part of a significant whole.

ANXIETY

Heidegger regards the experience of **anxiety** as a potentially 'enlightening' event. It can make a person re-evaluate their existence and see all the other possibilities available to them. In the mood of anxiety everything seems stripped of significance. Normally we identify with the 'stable' universe of our habitual thoughts, feelings, attitudes and material values, that are largely influenced by our absorption in the inauthentic *they-self*. This creates a sense of 'permanence' in our lives and hides the fact that our existence is founded on emptiness – it comes from nothing and returns to nothing. Consequently, there is no ultimate 'reason' for doing what we do, other than the reason we ourselves provide. The mood of anxiety is intensely disturbing because it reveals this *Nothingness* lying at the heart of human existence.

The strange feeling of anxiety, that one's consciousness will be completely and permanently terminated – that one will cease *to be* – cannot be compared to any other form of human experience; all other experiences exist in the continuum of time. It is not the *experience of dying* that is dreaded in the mood of anxiety, but our being able not-to-be – the fact that we become *Nothing*. This is the existential significance of this mood. As Heidegger says: 'The "nothing" with which anxiety brings us face to face, unveils the nullity by which *Dasein*, in its very *basis*, is defined; and this basis itself is as thrownness into death.'

Heidegger describes two ways of experiencing anxiety. The usual experience is an uneasy and indistinct background feeling, and the normal response to this is an escape into familiar everyday acitivities to block it out.

The other form of anxiety, which is far less frequent, is characterized by an unambiguous, intense and overwhelming sensation that disrupts our normal sense of existence. This mood reveals the naked truth about ourselves and the world, by stripping away all our familiar ways of perceiving things. Heidegger sees this experience as absolutely essential to the philosopher, since the detachment it provides from worldly concerns and prejudices is essential to philosophical thinking.

Because what anxiety reveals is so unsettling, we spend most of our lives trying to keep anxiety at bay. Our unreflective absorbtion in the *they-self*, with its numerous activities of everyday, prevents us from noticing the insecurity of life. According to Heidegger however, if we submit resolutely to what is revealed by anxiety, we can begin living authentically – accepting and assuming responsibility for our life and death. This is what Heidegger regards as true freedom.

The comfortable illusion of safety provided by our fallenness in the public 'they' is then broken when anxiety reveals that the 'they' can provide us neither with protection nor consolation from the constant possibility of our own death. Anxiety forces us to confront our mortality – we find ourselves staring directly into the void of Nothingness. We now find ourselves able to sense the temporal nature of our lives.

Anxiety can arise suddenly in any situation. For instance, I might be busy at work, or weeding the garden, or travelling home on the train when suddenly as if from nowhere I am ovewhelmed by the suffocating feeling that everything is meaningless and pointless. I may start to wonder 'What am I doing here?' 'Why do I bother with all this?' Whatever feeling of security I get from my normal everyday existence, from my achievements, belongings, my personal relationships and friendships – all this is completely shattered in an instant. This anxiety can be summarized as a deep *crisis* of meaning. I feel alienated from everything that ever seemed worthwhile to me. This mood makes existence seem inhospitable – the normally familiar things around me seem strange and unwelcoming. The complete detachment from everything in my life that is provided by the mood of anxiety allows me to dwell in the world clearsightedly and with resolution. I remember that my life is my own and that in each moment, it is up to me to make something of myself. I am then able to differentiate between what is, and isn't, important to me. Anxiety allows me to realize the shallowness of a self-concept based upon work, social status, achievements or material wealth, influenced by living as the *they-self*. So anxiety reveals the task of choosing who I am – it inspires me to make a change of course in my life. Alternatively, I may decide that what I am doing at the moment is in fact what I really most want to be doing – but now I am doing it out of personal choice.

So the mood of anxiety makes me aware of what *is*, by bringing me face to face with my *thrownness*. Heidegger emphasizes that the primordial meaning of anxiety is to feel not-at-home in the world. Since I no longer feel at-home as the *they-self*, living according to the superficial values of the *they-world*, I am forced to focus on my *own* Being, rather than the *they-self*. This *individualizes* me and reveals to me my *own* possibilities and the fact that my Being-in-the-world is rooted in a fundamental attitude of caring about my existence on all levels. I am now confronted with the choice between an authentic or inauthentic approach to existence.

CARE

'I care therefore I am' – though Heidegger did not actually say this, it expresses very appropriately the level of importance which Heidegger attaches to *Dasein*'s most fundamental feature. For it is **care** that makes human existence meaningful and makes a person's life *really* matter to them, and it is care which ultimately directs us to the mystery of Being itself.

Heidegger asserts that *all* the features that constitute *Dasein*'s Being-in-the-world in its average everydayness – *fallenness* (its absorption in the *they-world*), *Being-with* (its social context), *thrownness* (its living past) *moods* and *understanding* – are 'equiprimordial' and inseparable from one another. In other words, no single feature is a *derived* or *secondary addition*. Also, all features are simultaneously present in *Dasein*'s way of Being – no feature can exist without all the others also being present. But Heidegger points out that, since *Dasein*'s *fundamental* state is care, that all these features have their roots in, and are unified by, this primordial condition. In other words care embodies *Dasein* as a whole – it is the 'constellation' in which *Dasein* exists, the basic feature in us that constitutes all our involvements in the world, thus providing us with a sense of existence as an integrated 'organic' whole. It is care which potentially provides a cohesive, unifying structure to *Dasein*'s life that is necessary for an authentic, autonomous existence.

On a purely intuitional level it is easy to accept Heidegger's understanding of care, for there is an undercurrent of care in everything we do – in our interests, responsibilities, passions and disappointments, and especially when we are in a deeply introspective state of mind. In contrast, during the mood of extreme depression, which is the closest we come to lacking care, everything seems insignificant.

Heidegger explains that our manner of caring varies, depending upon the situation facing us. Our basic mode of caring is characterized by an attitude of worry or anxiety arising out of apprehension concerning our *own* Being and our *own* future possibilities.

Towards other people ('being-with-one-another') however, care takes the form of *solicitude* – taking care of, or providing for, the welfare of those in need of help. There are two types of solicitude: 'authentic' solicitude helps others to take responsibility for their own life, to stand on their own two feet and take care of themselves; 'dominating' inauthentic solicitude helps in a manner that reduces others to dependency.

During the practical activities of our job and daily life, in our use of machines, computers, tools or any other objects employed to achieve our aims, care becomes *concern* in the sense of 'attending to' or 'taking care of' the way we handle things (that which is ready-to-hand – *equipment*). Heidegger explains that when he uses the term 'care' this simultaneously includes the meanings *concern* and *solicitude*, in other words 'care' refers to 'concerned-solicitous care'. He points out that even when *Dasein* is neglectful, unconcerned or uncaring that care is still active, but in a 'deficient mode'.

Heidegger attaches great importance to the fact that *Dasein*'s 'care' embraces its past, present and future, for this shows that *Dasein*'s Being simultaneously occupies all three phases of time: in its *thrownness*, *Dasein* is already in the world, dealing with the *facticity* of its past; in its projection, it is focusing on and defining itself in terms of future possibilities; in its fallenness, *Dasein* is pre-occupied with the world in the *present*, involved with practical concerns as the *they-self*.

In other words, the unity of *Dasein* is grounded on *care*, which in turn is founded on temporality – the spanning of all the dimensions of time. So the past, present and future are 'alive' in every moment of human existence and constitute all our current actions. This is why Heidegger states that our existence and experience in time is *always already* three-dimensional. *Time* itself is therefore three-dimensional, since *Dasein's* way of Being reveals that past, present and future are a unity which cannot be divided.

The aspect of *Dasein's* way of Being-in-the-world that it most *cares* about is the fact that it is *alive*. When *Dasein* faces, during the identity crisis of deep anxiety, the inescapable fact that it may die at any time, it begins to *care* about its way of living in a far more intense and profound way. It now enters an authentic mode of existence, where what it *cares* about most of all is the fact that it is a Being-toward-death. If *Dasein's* basic state were not care, its mortality would not be experienced as being of paramount significance. In Heidegger's own words: 'I am this "I can die at any moment."… I myself am this constant and utmost possibility of myself, namely, to be no more. Care, which is essentially care about the Being of *Dasein*, at its innermost is nothing but this being-ahead-of-itself in the uttermost possibility of its own can-be'.

Being-towards-death

If you knew this would be the last day of your life, how would you spend it? Your answer says a lot about who you are – what you truly care about and the way you would really like to be living your life.

Death was a central theme of Heidegger's thought, throughout his entire philosophical career. The immense popularity of *Being and Time* owed much to his emphasis that a constant awareness and acceptance of the inevitability of one's own death was the essential foundation of authentic understanding. In a lecture in 1961 he asked rhetorically *where* we should go to reflect most effectively on the mystery of our origin. His answer was 'to the graveyard…' For Heidegger, it is the encounter with death that most profoundly highlights the question of Being. He says: 'Death opens up the question of Being … It is the shrine of Nothing and the shelter of Being.'

His detailed examination of human mortality, therefore, was motivated first and foremost by the question: 'What can death tell us about the fundamental meaning of Being?' And his findings are not at all a basis for morbidity and despair. On the contrary he asserts that his insights shed light on the fundamental significance of Being and provide the one essential key to personal freedom during one's lifetime.

Although he saw the 'question of death' as an essential part of any philosophical examination of life, he does not discuss the *final state* of death itself, nor does he comment on how one thinks, or should think, in the last moments just prior to death (where conditions are often not geared to reflection). The reason for this avoidance of any discussion of death itself, is that Heidegger realized that death is something we cannot experience – he shared the same attitude on this matter as stated by the philosopher Epicurus: 'If death is there, you aren't; if you are there, death isn't.' What is important to Heidegger, is that we are always on a one-way trip to death, and there is no escape. He used a medieval saying to express this: 'As soon as man enters on life, he is at once old enough to die.' And in his own words: 'This certainty, that "I myself *am* in that I will die", is *the basic certainty of Dasein itself.* It is a genuine statement of *Dasein* … *Dasein* exists as born; and, as born, it is already dying, in the sense of Being-towards-death.' What Heidegger investigates therefore, is not our actual demise, but our mortality – the fact that we are a *Being-towards-death.*

THE 'AFTERLIFE' ISSUE

Though he does not deny the possibility of an 'afterlife', Heidegger points out '… as long as I have not defined death in what it is, I cannot even rightly ask what could come after *Dasein* in connection with its death'. He clearly means here, that since he does not clarify what death *is* (because neither he nor anyone knows), then any discussion of an 'afterlife' *must* be irrelevant. He also would *not* have wished to speak further on this matter because it requires entering into the realm of theology – a field of inquiry which he regarded as completely inappropriate to proper philosophical thinking. So   Heidegger's analysis is not sourced in any traditional discussions of death.

HEIDEGGER'S 'FACTS OF LIFE' AND DEATH

All the choices I ever make are fundamentally rooted in who I already am. Whatever I choose in life simultaneously excludes numerous other possibilities. It is certain that I shall die. I may die at any time – death is a possibility that hangs over everything I do, at every moment. I will have to do my dying for myself because my death belongs *exclusively to me* – no one can do it for me or participate in my personal experience of it, and no one can take it away from me. Mortality is my *ownmost* possibility, because more than any other possibility it is *mine.* All the remaining possibilities in my life are potentially *avoidable* and open to others, but not *my* death. It is this which ultimately makes my life completely my own and this fact is a basic truth of the meaning of my

Being. Death is the ultimate evaluator, the end of everything, it will put an end to all my possibilities as I cannot do anything after I am dead. Death will sever all my relationships to others and complete the story of my life. The choices I make in life will be authentic only if they are based upon a clear awareness of these facts. To remain *unaware* of all this is what Heidegger terms an *inauthentic* 'fleeing in the face of death'.

As long as I am alive I am inhabited by what Heidegger calls 'a constant lack of totality' – a continual overhang of unfinished business owing to possibilities that still exist for me. A complete perspective on my life – the significance of my whole existence – can only be achieved when all of my possibilities are ended, but this only happens when my life is over and then of course I am not around to reflect upon it. So it appears from this that it will always be either *too early* or *too late* to see the *complete* picture of my existence.

DEATH AS A POSSIBILITY

Heidegger conceives death as *one of the possible ways of being*. This seems strange – contrary to logic which assumes that 'death and life cannot exist simultaneously'. But if *Dasein* is its not-yets, then death is clearly one of them. Until it occurs, it must exist now as a future possibility (albeit a certain one). So 'death is a way to be', but this fact is obscured by *Dasein*'s fallenness, in which it hides from death via an absorption in the everyday *they-world*. The inauthentic mood that discloses death is *fear* which focuses on the specific or actual event of death and flees from what it sees. This inauthentic attitude is characterized by a denial of the ever-present possibility of death – which is seen instead, as a remote possibility in the distant future that for the moment only happens to others. Though one may acknowledge that 'life is short, we don't live forever', the stinging significance of this is excluded from our feeling-awareness. This deprives *Dasein* of a sense of the totality of its own life. Heidegger states that the 'chattering' *they-self* 'does not allow us the courage for anxiety in the face of death'. When living inauthentically as the *they-self*, denial or self-deception allow an escape from the tremendous impact and significance of the inevitability of death.

Heidegger claims that to see death primarily as an actuality is an inauthentic perspective on death. The only meaningful way of viewing death is via the authentic realization that it is possible *not-to-be*, for this tends automatically to focus our attention on the possibility of being-able-to-be. Heidegger warns, however, against an inauthentic 'death-awareness' that is characterized by thinking about death (often obsessively and morbidly) in a manner that does not lead to a lifestyle characterized by authentic choices and based upon a genuine Being-towards-death. Additionally, though Heidegger did not mention suicide in *Being and Time*, he claims, in his later writings, that this is also an inauthentic or inappropriate response to the possibility of death.

Authentic awareness of death

Authentic awareness focuses on death as a constant possibility of our own Being rather than on the *actual event* of death itself. Heidegger asserts that when I experience myself always as this Being-towards-death, I am provided with a vantage point from where I am able to grasp my life as a whole. In the light of this awareness of death, I can see clearly now my present situation in life and the possibilities it offers me, for my awareness has released me from the grip of the *they* so I am now free to choose my own path in life. Heidegger describes the continuous background awareness of mortality as arising out of the mood of dread or anxiety which brings one face to face with the inevitability of one's own permanent extinction. Near-death experiences do not guarantee this state of awareness, as what is required is an *ontological* understanding of the matter, which requires the experience of dread toward the certainty of one's own death. Only when this happens is the authentic way of living made accessible. Truly feeling in the depths of your Being that each moment may be your last, frees you from pettiness, and the pressures of living as others expect you to live. You can then realize the deeper significance of existence.

Whereas inauthentic *Dasein* tends to be completely absorbed in the present and the immediate past and future, authentic *Dasein* looks ahead to its death, back to its birth and beyond, to its historical past in order to survey its own life as a whole.

According to Heidegger, the constant realization of the inevitability of one's own death, which can occur at any time, is therefore an essential condition of human freedom. Death confirms and reveals the sobering truth that the essence and meaning of human life is grounded in time. The possibilities of my life are defined by, dependent on, and only make sense in the light of my eventual death.

5 Conscience, guilt and authenticity

CONSCIENCE

Heidegger does not focus on the traditional moral, ethical, or religious views of conscience or guilt, but offers a fundamental, existential interpretation that sheds further light on our way of Being. He claims that we need the special moments of insight provided by the conscience, to open us to authentic understanding. His inquiry is rooted in how the 'call' of conscience is focused on and highlights the conflict between *Dasein*'s two contrasting ways of Being:

* The 'they-self' in which *Dasein* is absorbed in the present, preoccupied with the concerns of everyday reality, where the choices it makes, the way it thinks and all of its behaviour is under the influence of the 'they';

* The 'homeless' self – the source of conscience.

In this part of its Being, *Dasein* is experiencing a sense of anxiety or dread, that arises from the awareness of having been *thrown* naked into a seemingly meaningless existence. It has lost that comfortable feeling of belonging with the crowd and feels instead like 'a stranger in a strange world'. It is this part of *Dasein* which functions as a primordial **conscience**, silently reaching out or 'calling' to that part of itself which exists under the influence of the 'they'. It tries to make the 'they-self' realize it can choose its *own* possibilities, rather than conforming to the restricted possibilities offered by the 'they'. In appealing to the fallen 'they-self' to become an individualized authentic self, the call of conscience reveals to *Dasein* its own *primordial* guilt. Not everyone responds to this call and no one responds all the time. Often when the conscience reminds us of our potential for authenticity we prefer to turn away from this awareness back into the security of the 'they-self' in order to escape the heavy burden of facing up to the responsibility of authentic Being. Yet, the call of conscience is always hovering on the periphery of awareness, destined to return on other occasions when perhaps we will choose to respond to its appeal.

GUILT

The **guilt** Heidegger discusses has nothing to do with our normal understanding and use of that term. Instead, he refers to the type of guilt which is a primordial part of our essential way of Being as 'care': 'entities whose Being is care ... are guilty in the very basis of their Being.'

He asserts that every *Dasein* is always essentially guilty, but *Dasein*, when in the mode of the 'they-self', lives in denial of this guilt. In the authentic mode of Being however, *Dasein* realizes its guilt and bases its actions on a full awareness of it.

According to Heidegger, *Dasein* is existentially guilty because his very Being is built upon '*not*-ness'. As *Dasein*, my guilt is inherent in the structure of 'care' which embraces both past and future dimensions of my Being. I am guilty for having a *past* based on 'notness' due to my *thrownness* which I do not control. Yet this must serve as the basis for my existence – I am *not* responsible for my entry into the world, nor the circumstances into which I was born. I cannot change what I have been up till now. What I become will always, in some way, be based upon my past. I also bear existential guilt because on the basis of my past I choose possibilities for my *future,* but I have no rules and no intrinsic nature to guide me, as in essence I consist of pure, naked, 'homeless' possibility that is 'rooted' in the void of 'notness' – Nothingness.

In addition I choose possibilities for my future that are *not* other possibilities. I am fundamentally responsible for the choices I make which determine who I am, and each time I choose one possibility I am also choosing to *ignore* other possibilities, so I am always actualizing one possible self, at the expense of many others, which may be equally worthwhile. Our guilty indebtedness to these other possible selves is thus a fundamental feature of existence. It reveals my ontological *finitude* – the fact that I cannot be all that I could be.

Authentic choices will often be swimming against the current of expectations from the 'they'. All choices I make have unforeseen consequences for which I am ultimately responsible. Most importantly, when I choose my fundamental way of Being for my whole life, I cannot justify this particular choice rather than another equally relevant choice. In other words, choosing or preferring one particular way of life is based upon the rejection of all the other equally valid available choices.

In everyday existence *Dasein* is absorbed in the present and does not acknowledge its guilt. Only authentic *Dasein* realizes its guilt and acts in full awareness of it. So conscience is asking us to *own up* to our guilt and to make our actions our *own*, and in doing this we can exist authentically. *Dasein*'s guilt is uniquely its own, because it is free to accept or reject its possibilities. Like facing death, this acceptance of guilt requires confronting the truth of our own fragile existence, acknowledging the *guilt* that our existence is 'as an entity which has to be as it is and as it can be'. Heidegger asserts that when we own up to guilt, we gain **resoluteness** which is the fundamental mind-set of authenticity. The resolute man is guilty, he knows he is guilty, and he wants to have a conscience. In other words, when *Dasein* truly understands the nature of his conscience and his guilt, he becomes resolute.

AUTHENTICITY

Heidegger describes two fundamentally different ways in which human beings can understand and live their lives – **authentic** and **inauthentic**. The authentic way allows for a far deeper experience of the significance of existence. Heidegger's discussion of these two modes is an essential part of his inquiry into *Dasein*'s way of Being-in-the-world. His use of these terms allows him to differentiate between the ways in which the meaning of our existence is revealed to us or concealed from us. His aim is not to try to change anyone or preach morals – but to help provide insights that shed more light on the question of Being. Authenticity refers to a mode of existence in which I am aware of my *own* self and my *own* possibilities, and thus I choose my *own* way of life. When I am inauthentic, I am *not* aware of my own self or my own possibilities. This distinction is applicable to every single possible way in which I exist. For example, if I think authentically, I can learn something truthful about the meaning of my existence, but this does not happen when I think inauthentically.

Although the 'inner voice' of human beings calls for authenticity and self-fulfilment, Heidegger makes it clear that becoming an authentic being is not a 'return' to an 'original self' that I *used* to be, since the inauthentic 'they-self' has been my identity from the beginning. Instead, the process involves a struggle to win my freeedom from the all-pervasive domination of this 'they-self', and what is left will be my authentic self, experienced for the first time.

To be authentic is to be true to my *own* self, to be my *own* person, to do my *own* thing, regardless of the opinion of the 'they'. But this depends on the most fundamental characteristic of authenticity – an awareness of my *own* possibilities in the light of the finite nature of my existence. This can only arise out of the mood of anxiety, which can help me to recognize the unique wholeness of my Being. In this mood a deep awareness of my own mortality leads me to the realization that I am at all times a Being-towards-death. I now understand that I (and not the *they*) am responsible for my own death, which means ultimately I also must be responsible for my own life. I now *care* authentically about my existence. Heidegger emphasizes, however, that authentic living is not about detachment, changing the content of the *world*, or breaking contact with others, for our own existence is inseparable from the *world* I share with others. The authentic choices I make may, or may not, result in an alteration of the *actual content* of my life – for the only relevant matter here becomes the fact that I am now exercising freedom of choice. Whatever I now choose to do with my life – even if this is exactly what I have been doing up till now – is my own free choice uninfluenced by the expectations of others. So the *form* of my life (living as a Being-towards-death rather than as the 'they-self') is changed, whilst the *actual content* – my particular *world* and life – in a sense becomes irrelevant. Although I will still remain under the influence of the 'they' in certain fundamental ways – as in everyday practical concerns – and will be limited by, and dependent upon, the range of available possibilities offered by my *world*, I nevertheless have freedom *within* this context to make my *own* choices, as I no longer take the familiar expectations of the 'they' as 'the only game in town'. In choosing to live as a Being-towards-death, exhibiting care towards my *world* I have become *resolute* – Heidegger regards **resoluteness** as the essential and key feature of authenticity.

He does not discuss whether or not resolute choices can be wrong. There are no rules by which we can decide for ourselves or for others what has to be done. There are no objectively correct answers to life's basic problems and there are no objective criteria that Heidegger offers for determining the rightness or wrongness of a choice. The best one can do is to to make one's choices resolutely whilst keeping the totality of one's whole life and the certainty of death in clear perspective. And there is no remedy for the fact that when I make a choice now that seems to be good, it may turn out to have negative consequences. For Heidegger, resoluteness is not morally superior to **irresoluteness**. Resolute individuals do not necessarily behave in a morally superior way – for instance, Mahatma Gandhi was resolute, but so was Adolf Hitler. So, although authenticity requires resoluteness, this does not mean that a resolute person will be authentic. The 'virtue' of resoluteness as a way of Being is that it enables one potentially to become aware of one's own possibilities and wholeness, in a way that irresoluteness does not.

Heidegger claims that most of us are irresolute most of the time. When irresolute *Dasein* has a job to do, it concentrates on that, without questioning whether what it is doing is a fitting way to spend one's time. Lost in the 'they-self', it is completely absorbed in the present or the immediate past and future in a manner which ignores its own future possibilities. In contrast, if I am resolute I survey my life by traversing the totality of its past, present and future. Heidegger explains that authentic *Dasein* 'runs ahead' into the future to experience the impact of the inevitability of its own death and then 'backwards' beyond its birth to assess its own individual and historical past. So it knows that its normal everyday existence, into which it has been thrown, is only one possible set of circumstances amongst many, for its life is rooted in the larger drama of our shared cultural history and its possibilities therefore arise from the 'wellsprings' of a 'heritage' from previous generations.

Authentic *Dasein* thus relates to the future in terms of the choices that it can make between its own possibilities, and it *anticipates* the future by *going towards* it. By contrast, inauthentic *Dasein* relates to the future merely by waiting to see the results, the success or failure of the current activity or situation – the *possible future outcome* of events, circumstances and affairs of everyday projects – it *waits* for the future to *come towards* it.

To sum up, the authentic perspective provided by my death awareness snatches me out of the grip of the 'they-self', and frees me from a multitude of comfortable, but shallow, inauthentic possibilities it offers. Instead I follow my *own* path through life by making my own free choices based on the awareness that I am a Being-towards-death. My existence has now become *individualized.* I no longer blame anyone else for what happens in my life as I am resolute – I thus take charge of my life as a whole with decisive dedication towards what I want to accomplish. My stance towards the future is one of clear-sighted anticipation based upon a total commitment to the fundamental direction I have *freely* chosen in life. This way of living lends a sense of cohesiveness and integrity to my existence. My actions become an expression of what I really want to be doing with my life as they are now based upon my *own* choices rather than upon the expectations of others.

The 'Truth of *Aletheia*' and Language

6

Philosophy is the search for truth. Heidegger claimed that essentially there are two main approaches to truth. The traditional one, which has existed since its introduction by Plato, claims that truth can be defined in terms of specific *criteria* for assessing true or false propositions. In contrast to this, Heidegger investigates the *meaning* or *essence* of truth, that exists independently of, and prior to, any criteria. Truth in his sense of the word is not merely a presentation of static facts, but a process that is alive and happening in each moment. For Heidegger such 'truth' is the essential foundation of all knowledge.

TRADITIONAL CONCEPTS OF TRUTH

The standard definition of truth used today, is the **correspondence theory** which requires statements to be verified or 'proven' by the 'facts' – judgements, statements or propositions are correct or true only if they factually 'match' the object or situation they are referring to. A proposition is either true or it is not. There are no degrees or graduations of truth or untruth. In all such systems, truth is something that occurs only within the perimeter of specific 'rules' or 'conditions' that are used for its assessment and meanwhile, according to Heidegger, the question of what truth actually *is*, or what it *means*, is completely ignored.

Heidegger noted that such views of truth tend to place humanity 'at the centre of the universe', in terms of controlling all definitions of truth/falseness and right/wrong. He regarded this attitude as the source of our technological outlook that causes us to regard the planet simply as a vast resource, exclusively for our benefit. So it is of central importance to Heidegger that *Dasein* understands that truth cannot be understood merely via the assimilation of knowledge derived from 'true' propositions. This futile attempt to know life via theories, offers 'truths' that provide a severely narrowed perspective on reality. 'True sentences' are merely true sentences, but the primary ground of truth is in actual existence which resides in the living process of existence itself, as it is unfolding.

So Heidegger's approach is not a theory, but rather an analysis of truth – he investigates what actually happens in situations where truth occurs. This is radically different from any approaches used by philosophers before him. Truth is no longer the relationship between a subject-knower and the object-known, instead it is something that is *occurring*. And what is occurring is that the *meaning* of an event is revealed to us. The immediate and obvious advantage of such an approach is that unlike the previously mentioned traditional systems of truth, Heidegger's way makes it possible to investigate the meaning of Being itself, rather than merely the entities that arise out of Being.

HEIDEGGER'S TRUTH OF *ALETHEIA*

Heidegger claimed that all types of 'propositional truths' are derived from this more primordial and far deeper truth, which he called *aletheia*. This is the ancient Greek word for 'truth' – the root or original meaning is 'unconcealment'. So the Greeks (and Heidegger) saw truth as an uncovering, disclosing, revealing or unveiling of something, rather than the agreement between a thought or statement and its object – in other words, truth occurs when something is revealed.

Heidegger believed that for us to really know or experience any entity (including ourselves) as it really is, it first has to be revealed to us – unconcealed. He regarded such disclosure as the essence of truth from which all other theories and uses of truth are derived. For instance, the traditional view of truth is, in comparison, extremely shallow and limited because all the 'components' of this truth (the statements or judgements, the objects they refer to and the statement maker) are themselves 'entities' that first have to be recognized as such, prior to any 'matching up'.

To make this point clearer, in his later works, Heiddegger describes a hierarchy of *three* levels of truth – *propositional* truth is the lowest of these and dependent on the other two. He illustrates this via the statement 'the picture is askew on the wall' – confirmation of the truth of this proposition is only possible because of *ontic truth* (factual information), which reveals the fact that the picture is, quite obviously, hanging crookedly. Heidegger sees ontic truth as the first stage of unconcealment. But the picture can reveal itself to us as hanging askew only because of *ontological truth* (the highest level) in which the event of our existence is revealed – in other words, *Dasein* first needs *to exist* in order for the crookedness of the picture to matter and be noticed. So *aletheia* – unconcealment – is clearly a prerequisite for the application of the 'correspondence theory' (and all other theories) of truth. Heidegger therefore saw *aletheia* as the fundamental truth.

However, entities also need some *place* where their unconcealment can occur. In *Being and Time* that place was *Dasein*. Entities were 'disclosed' (unconcealed or revealed) to *Dasein* via the process of direct, and primarily practical, experience. For instance, the Being or 'hammerness' of a hammer was disclosed whilst *Dasein* was using it for its intended purpose, or alternatively an event such as rain 'revealed itself' in the presence of *Dasein*'s passive, but interested, awareness of it.

For Heidegger then, truth occurs each time that the meaning of an event is revealed to *us*, and *Dasein* is a being that always remains receptive to experiencing the truth of other beings. Heidegger viewed this receptiveness as a 'clearing' – an 'open space' in which entities could manifest themselves. He said that *Dasein* itself *is* this 'clearing'. According to Heiddeger, truth is therefore a characteristic of *Dasein* and dependent on *Dasein*. This conclusion led to his statement that truth exists only so long as *Dasein* exists – there is no truth without *Dasein*.

It is important to note here that Heidegger does not mean that *Dasein* *determines* what truth *is*. However, since truth is defined as unconcealment, based on disclosure, and since entities need the 'open clearing' of *Dasein* in order to reveal (disclose) themselves, then logically, truth can exist only as part of *Dasein*'s mode of existence as an entity that provides this clearing for disclosure. *Dasein* is therefore an entity 'in truth'. This claim is also consistent with traditional theories – without propositions there would be no truth, and since *we* makes the propositions, how could there be truth without us. Heidegger adds that, because of *Dasein*'s *fallenness,* it always contains closed-off or unexpressed 'hidden' possibilities, so *Dasein* is always in part 'hidden' or concealed. Consequently, *Dasein* is described by Heidegger as being simultaneously in 'truth' *and* 'untruth': 'Truth is un-truth, insofar as there belongs to it the reservoir of the not-yet-uncovered, in the sense of concealment.'

In terms of conventional thinking, in which things are either true or false, this idea of the co-existence of truth and untruth seems absurd. Understood in Heidegger's sense however the statement makes perfect sense. Truth is constantly in the process of uncovering what is still concealed in it and this activity never ends, which is why in *Dasein*'s case and in all other situations, 'truth is always simultaneously in untruth'. This whole discussion crystallizes in Heidegger's claim that an understanding of *Dasein*'s way of Being is the fundamental foundation of truth – the disclosure of *Dasein* via its own relentless inquiry to reveal itself as it exists is what truth *means.*

In his later writings, however, Heidegger saw the vastness of *Being* itself, rather than *Dasein,* as *the* 'clearing'. He describes this place as an 'open region' or 'field of relatedness', where entities manifest themselves and interact in varying ways, and although humans are not in power here, they are still of fundamental importance. Heidegger speaks of this open region as the place that 'illuminates' the 'presence' of entities – where *Dasein* experiences the unconcealment or 'truth' of an entity's presence or Being.

Heidegger points out however, that in order to understand the most fundamental events of Being we should realize that this clearing is not a clearly definable place, but rather an infinitely complex area of *possibilities*. In it, all beings cannot be disclosed simultaneously – they may or *may not* appear.

The concept of *aletheia* contains at the same time both unconcealment *and* concealment. Paradoxically, it is unconcealment that produces this concealment. This idea can be grasped quite easily, if one thinks about how a radio functions; tuning into one wavelength, automatically and simultaneously blocks out all other wavelengths, but these other channels, nevertheless, remain as unheard possibilities. Similarly, when an entity is revealed in one particular way, this simultaneously conceals all the remaining possible ways of its Being. Thinking about truth in this way opens up a very flexible view of truth in which something can express *degrees* of unconcealment, like a landscape seen in the half-light of dawn. The clarity of truth, in this sense, often emerges only gradually, similar to the process of discovering meaning in true works of art, whose deeper significance is not immediately apparent.

So there is a great deal of ambiguity in this 'clearing' he describes – every unconcealment, automatically resulting in concealment. But for Heidegger, this *is* the truth of Being – an endless cycle of the unveiling-veiling of entities in existence. This process even seems to be hinted at in his choice of the Greek word *aletheia*, which contains the word *lethe*, meaning 'forgetfulness'.

In *Being and Time* Heidegger discusses how truth can be seen in the disclosure of the 'meaning' of ordinary everyday events and things. In his later works he adds that 'the essence of truth is the truth of essence'. Here he is offering the additional insight that truth as the unconcealment or disclosure of what it means to be, can only be found via the uncovering of 'essences'. Heidegger's term 'essence' has nothing to do with the traditional idea of essence as a single, covering definition. His concept refers instead to 'that which makes something what it is' – in other words *Being*. So the 'truth of essence' therefore means the uncovering of the meaning of Being which is also the intrinsic 'meaning' of any entity.

HEIDEGGER'S CONCEPT OF LANGUAGE

More than any philosopher before him, Heidegger was preoccupied with the overwhelming influence that language exerted on human thought. In one of his later essays, 'A dialogue on Language', he writes: 'Language is the House of Being. Man dwells in this house ... In language there occurs the revelation of beings ... In the power of language man becomes the witness of Being ... Man is the shepherd of Being.' It is clear from such statements that Heidegger regarded language as not only tied up with daily human existence, but also with Being, which discloses itself to and in man *via language.*

In contrast to this though, he felt that language was potentially very dangerous, because a silent world is simply what it is, whereas a world experienced through, or represented by, language is radically unstable and open to multiple and conflicting interpretations. 'Because man *is* in language, he creates this danger and brings the destruction it threatens.' He saw this destructiveness as visible in the current decayed state of communication – 'superficial idle talk' predominates, resulting in a forgetfulness of Being that causes an inauthentic relationship with existence.

THE EMPTINESS OF EVERYDAY LANGUAGE

Heidegger observed that words in general had become impotent – worn out and emptied of meaning from overuse and thus unfit for 'thinking Being' in depth. For instance, look at how the word 'love' is used today: 'I love beer ... I love football ... see you later love...'. Add to this the appearance of the word on thousands of shirts, greeting cards and commercials and it comes as no surprise to learn that the word has now been sucked dry of the original meaning and intensity it once had. According to Heidegger this was not always the case. There was a time when the word 'love' was first used when no difference existed between the word and the intense feeling of loving emotion that it was expressing. Around the time of its birth, each time the word was spoken there existed simultaneously the real experience of love. For

Heidegger, the key to understanding ourselves lies in recognizing and re-living the initial moments of existence when 'Being first spoke' to us through fundamentally important words like 'peace', 'love', 'truth' and 'compassion'. When this happens, someone who says 'I love you' will truly experience the original significance of these words and their behaviour will reflect their experience.

THE LANGUAGE OF BEING

Heidegger constructed a new vocabulary and style of expression attuned specifically to Being. He developed a unique and complex way of expressing ideas which involved the usage of obsolete words, personal spellings (such as the archaic spelling **Seyn** ('Being') instead of **Sein**), multiple resonances, brand new words and strange verbal constructions. He created dozens of hyphenated compound words that in their original German, end with the word -*sein* meaning '-being', and he introduced the word *Dasein* to refer to 'us'. This attachment of the German word for 'Being' throughout his writing continually brings the reader back to Heidegger's primary question – the *meaning* of Being.

He felt that this new way of expressing philosophical concepts would regenerate the language, stimulate a fresh, new perspective on existence and make us think radically about who we are. The increased effort required to comprehend his unusual style also results in a far deeper understanding of its content.

However, it is important to remember that his terminology, though unusual, is sometimes far easier to understand in its original language than when it is translated into English – Heidegger plays with etymological family relationships that exist only in the German language. Indeed, though he praised translations of his work *Being and Time*, he considered efforts to translate his later writings a waste of time, as their meaning was so totally dependent and exclusive to German and its linguistic past. Some of Heidegger's writing is definitely very obscure and ambiguous – even to native Germans with a fair measure of philosophic literacy. What makes things more difficult is that he often altered the meanings he originally attributed to certain words. Perhaps the most obvious example of this occurs with the word *Dasein*. In *Being and Time* one of the primary meanings of *Dasein* is 'being-there' in which 'there' refers to (being) *in-the-world*. When using this same term in his later writings, 'there' refers to where Being actually *is* – the *dwelling-place* of Being. He usually indicates this sense, by hyphenating *Da-sein*.

He defends these 'inconsistencies', as well as his other unique, unclear linguistic constructions, by pointing out that language becomes dull and lifeless when it is merely a fixed, unchanging, unambiguous tool for communicating information and classifying entities. Also, Heidegger sometimes felt forced to pioneer new and strange uses of language because the linguistic means to express his ideas did not exist. A typical and notable example of this occurred in one of his lectures when he declared: 'As I live in an environment, it signifies to me overall and always, 'it worlds''… His listeners were struck by the phrase *es weltet*, 'it worlds' or 'it is worlding'. Perhaps this suggests that Heidegger was trying to express succinctly and creatively that he experienced the world around him as a constantly changing 'living' organism.

ANCIENT GREEK AND GERMAN

A major tool in Heidegger's renovation of language was his use of ancient Greek. He considered this to be the primordial, original language of Europe, most rooted in the experience of Being. Because of this special relationship to entities and to Being, Heidegger describes Greek as the **logos** – a language in which the words are inseparable from what they name. According to Heidegger, German was directly descended from ancient Greek. He claimed that other European languages were either derivatives of German or contaminated by the 'deforming conduit' of the dead language Latin – thus disconnected from the their roots, the 'umbilical cord' of Being. He believed this meant that Germany had a unique national asset of privileged access to this Greek experience of Being.

Heidegger asserted that 'through the audible Greek word we are directly in the presence of the thing itself, not first in the presence of a mere word-sign'. He saw the Greek language as an 'extended memory of Being' where certain words were like a tape recording of the very first moment a human underwent a particular experience of existence. In reviving the usage of such words, the essence and energy of this original experience can be recaptured. He believed a resuscitation of this language could catalyse what he called 'the other beginning' – a new era of evolved thinking.

He also explored his own language, searching out in particular earlier meanings of words which had connotations of 'being'. For instance, **bauen** is the German verb meaning 'to build', but he replaced this sense of the word with the Old German usage which meant 'nurturing, cultivating, preserving and caring' – words more closely related to Being than to technical construction.

TALK – THE BASIS OF LANGUAGE

In his discussion of language in *Being and Time*, Heidegger maintains that *talking*, rather than grammatical properties or logic, is the essential basis of language. First there is the live action of talking – relevant here is the identity and personality of speaker and listener, their relationship and the circumstances and nature of the interaction. The means used to express the *talking* is language. Then later, when interpreted theoretically, language becomes words and sentences. Words and sentences are derived from a prior reality and as such do not carry with them the foundation of communication (which is talk). This was why Heidegger was fond of saying that statements may be 'correct but not true'. Any relevant authentic discussion of written language must take into account the complete circumstances of the original live action of *talking*.

Since 'talk' is the basis of language, Heidegger considers the activities of 'keeping silent' and of 'hearing' as being of the greatest relevance – they are a fundamental part of the process of talking and therefore an indispensable part of the structure of language. Consequently, mere words and sentences cannot effectively represent language in terms of the original 'live' process of talking. This is why, in the process of reading a novel, the skilled reader is not merely a viewer of the words on the page. He or she contributes their own 'talk', which makes them feel like an active participant of the written content. This brings to life the events in the book via a filling-in of the unspoken components of the real-life circumstances being described. It is only when this existential mode of 'talking' takes place that one can really gain some sense of the reality being expressed in words and sentences.

LANGUAGE – OUR PRIMARY ACCESS TO BEING

Although in *Being and Time* Heidegger regards language fundamentally as a means of interaction and communication between human beings in an already-established world, he explains in his later writings that the *primordial* and most important function of language is 'projective'. Language names entities for the first time, thus giving us something that we can talk about – for if a thing has no name it clearly cannot be discussed. Heidegger strongly disputes the common view that we are the 'creators' of language. He claims instead that 'language speaks, not man. Man only speaks when he fatefully answers to language.' It is 'the word' that first brings a thing into its 'is' and lets a thing be as a thing'. In other words, language *brings* beings *into* existence, in the sense that prior to 'naming' entities may *exist*, but not in the same way as they exist after they have been named. By 'establishing' and 'preserving' beings through the action of 'naming', language thus *enables* our primary access to Being.

THE SILENT 'SAYING' OF THE WORLD

The 'language' Heidegger is speaking of here has nothing to do with the conventional understanding of the word. He explains that all entities in existence, including all forms of conventional language, can best be understood as the expression of a primordial language – a kind of 'saying' – which is the essence of language prior to all known forms of language and speech. He explains how our familiar environment allows us to understand and assimilate a knowledge of certain skills – for instance, fishing – without our needing to use speech, or language derived from speech. This indicates there is *meaning* inherent in our world that exists *prior* to language. It is this process of transmission of meaning that he refers to when he speaks of the world 'saying' something to us. This 'saying' is obviously silent or mute because there is no perceivable 'act' of communication. So Heidegger perceived the meaningfulness of the world as a kind of silent 'saying' and he described the relationship of human beings to that 'saying' as one of 'hearing'.

In his later writings on language, Heidegger assigns great importance to this notion of hearing and claims that human speech is always, and necessarily, preceded by a 'hearing' in this sense. This is a 'hearing' of the 'saying' in which presence is realized; and because language in the widest sense *is* this *presence* and this *saying*, Heidegger states not only that 'language itself speaks' but that 'we hear the speaking of language'. So he is claiming that this language, which is prior to all human expression and communication, is a language rooted *in the world* and spoken to us *by the world*. He later spoke of 'Being' itself, as the fundamental *voice* of language. In spite of this radical assertion that language is prior to human speech, he acknowledges that the relationship is reciprocal, since without language man could not be man any more than language could be language. He says that this 'prior language' is dependent on human speech, but not *created* by human speech or under man's control.

THE LANGUAGE OF POETRY

Heidegger concluded that: 'The essence of Being is never conclusively sayable. The most we can do is try to think along with the poet who, hearing what is said in the silent Saying of language, can compose it into a poetry that awakens a renewed experience of the truth of Being.' Heidegger believed the language of poetry to be the *deepest* revelation of what *is*, because it reveals the *beingness* of beings and thus is potentially *more real* than reality itself as it discloses the essence of 'ordinary' things that normally we do not notice. 'Poetic language brings what *is*, as it *is*, into the Open for the first time.' Poetry carries the energy that was inherent in language when ancient Greek first named things – at that time, all language *was* poetry. When language recaptures this illuminating power, it lets us see the world as if for the first time, and it is *this* which Heidegger regards as true poetry. Inspired by this view of poetry, Heidegger began to use a 'language of metaphor' unique to him – attaching brand new meanings to simple words such as 'sky' and 'earth' – and his philosophic speech became what linguists call an 'ideolect', the idiom of an individual.

7

Tao, Zen and Heidegger

Over the past couple of decades, there have been a number of authors who have written on Heidegger's philosophy, who have recognized, especially in his later thought, a certain affinity with East Asian philosophy, most notably with Taoism and Zen Buddhism. Heidegger acknowledged this connection himself. In one of his essays, 'Conversation with a Japanese', he suggests that there is a possible rapport between his own thinking and Japanese philosophy. On another occasion he wrote of the 'resonances' between the Chinese term *Tao* and his own notion of *Ereignis* – the spontaneous arising and interconnectedness of all things in which truth is self-evident.

The fact that the Japanese have published seven translations of *Being and Time* also suggests that there may be a distinct compatibility between Heidegger's thought and East Asian philosophy.

TAOISM AND HEIDEGGER

In the book *Heidegger's Hidden Sources: East Asian influences on his work*, the author, Reinhard May, suggests that Taoism is in fact a 'hidden source' of Heidegger's thought. It is clear however, from the available biographical facts, that Heidegger did not take any formal courses in Eastern philosophy, nor did he promote or talk to any extent about meditation, spiritual training or enlightenment. Nevertheless a philosopher of Heidegger's calibre – like many other German-speaking philosophers of his generation – would undoubtedly, in his early studies, have come across German versions of the *Tao Te Ching*.

A reliable commentator of Heidegger noted that in 1930 Heidegger cited a famous passage from Chuang-Tsu, to help settle a debate on the nature of intersubjectivity. Later, in 1946, he chose to spend most of the summer working with a Chinese student (Paul Shih-yi Hsiao) on

translating sections of the *Tao Te Ching*. Although he did not complete
this task, one can nevertheless assume from his initial interest in the
project that he must have had a fairly in-depth knowledge of this
masterwork of Eastern Oriental philosophy.

Whether or not this influenced his thought is clearly a matter for
speculation, however, there are definitely clear parallels between
aspects of Taoism and Heidegger's manner of thinking. In Taoism, the
Tao (often translated 'Way') encompasses both the cosmic and human
realm of experience. The 'Way' is described as the source of the cosmos
and everything in existence – the weather, mountains, rivers, plants,
animals and human beings. Similarly, Heidegger cites 'Being' as the
essence of *Dasein* – it is also the primordial condition or fundamental
ground that allows everything else in the universe to come into
existence.

The *Tao* is always in the midst of change and can only be understood
in this context. Heidegger describes 'Being' as a continually evolving
phenomenon and *Dasein*'s structure is temporal – inextricably linked
to the passage of time.

Taoist philosophy explains that the *Tao* cannot be expressed in abstract
concepts. In *Being and Time*, dissatisfied with the results of his
discussion of Being, he stated that words cannot explain the 'isness' of
Being, which is 'intrinsically mysterious and self-concealing', and that
attempts to define it or subject it to logical analysis are like 'reaching
into a void'. He concluded that all one could say about it verbally was
'Being is Being'.

The *Tao* can only be interpreted through direct experience, and
figuratively through such means as imagery. The prominence of water
imagery, used to hint at aspects of the 'Way' in Taoist philosophy, seems
to parallel the images of Nature used in Heidegger's lectures on the
poet Holderlin. Also, the ideal Taoist state of mind, which is one of
contemplation defined by a 'let things be as they are' attitude to

existence, seems to correspond closely with Heidegger's description of the attitude of 'abandonment' – in which one adapts to the way things are in their ceaseless, flowing becoming.

ZEN AND HEIDEGGER

 If your mind is empty, it is always ready for anything; it is open to everything. In the beginner's mind there are many possibilities; in the expert's mind there are few.

(Shunryu Suzuki: *Zen Mind, Beginner's Mind*)

This fundamental view of the 'beginner's mind' in Zen Buddhism is clearly echoed in a letter written by Heidegger to a former teacher in 1928: 'Perhaps philosophy shows most forcibly and persistently how much Man is a beginner. Philosophizing ultimately means nothing other than being a beginner.'

In his search for an understanding of the question of Being, Heidegger turned to the *beginnings* of philosophy in Greece, whilst searching in the present for the place in which philosophy is always being born *anew.* He also often talked in terms of 'the new beginning' with reference to the change in thought that he hoped could emerge as a result of his new approach to thinking.

Heidegger's description of the experience of authenticity has much in common with Zen Buddhist enlightenment. Where Zen speaks of the 'pure experience' or the 'experience of nothingness' as *satori* or enlightenment, Heidegger describes how intense anxiety can open us to a profound awareness of Nothingness, that can in turn potentially lead to an authentic mode of existence.

A famous Zen story about the 'stages' of enlightenment states: 'Before enlightenment occurs, mountains are mountains; at the moment of enlightenment, mountains cease being mountains; but then mountains become mountains again.' The similarity to Heidegger's thinking seems clear: For Heidegger, prior to living authentically one exists according to everyday practices. When we allow anxiety to reveal that we are 'Being-towards-death' – rooted in 'Nothingness' – everyday practices slide away into meaninglessness; afterward, one resumes everyday practices once again, but this time guided by an awareness of our own possibilities rather than by the expectations of the 'they'.

Like Zen enlightenment, Heidegger's state of authenticity requires no faith in or experience of God. Also, he claims that the mind is more receptive to the 'astonishing mystery of Being' whilst it is completely absorbed in the single question 'what is the meaning of Being?' This is reminiscent of the *Koan* approach to enlightenment used in the Rinzai sect of Zen where the student meditates on a question that has no logical answer such as 'What is the sound of one hand clapping?'

Heidegger's authentic approach to life shares many qualities with the enlightened Zen way of living. Both arise spontaneously following a realization of the non-dualistic nature of existence that releases the individual from the illusion that they are a separate independent ego living in a world disconnected from all other apparently independent entities. Similarly Heidegger and Zen are both in agreement that this ending of a dualistic perception of existence allows us to see immediately the interconnected and mutually dependent nature of all beings in this unified existence. This insight is evident in the 'all is one' realization of Zen and in the expressions from Heidegger's *Being and Time,* which describe *Dasein* as 'being-in-the-world' and 'being-with-others'.

In addition, the enlightened Zen state recognizes that the apparent 'solidity' of the things we encounter in the world is illusory, as all things in reality are 'empty' and impermanent. Heidegger obviously agrees with this point as he praises Socrates for 'remaining continually in the powerful "draft" of direct experience which constantly evaporates and undermines the *presumed solidity* of the familiar everyday world'. Zen is aware of the suffering created as a result of our futile attempts to make the Nothingness, or emptiness, that we are into something enduring. Heidegger sees this condition as 'inauthentic living' and points out that liberation from this is only possible if *Dasein* finally realizes that it is intrinsically a Being-towards-death.

Both authentic understanding and Zen enlightenment intensify what had previously been only partially experienced. For instance, Heidegger describes a full flowering of the state of 'care', and in Zen there is the emergence of deepened compassion – both of these states provide a sense of profound significance to existence. In Heidegger and Zen, primary importance is placed upon the ordinary actions of everyday life. Heidegger emphasizes that authentic understanding can arise only out of our intimate *practical* interaction with our world and the entities in it. He regards this as *Dasein*'s primordial way of relating to, and understanding, reality. For instance we cannot truly know the nature of a hammer by 'objectively' analysing it – only via our wholehearted *use* of it. This attitude is epitomized in Zen by the great reverence paid by practitioners to apparently mundane activities such as making tea: in the 'tea-ceremony' the procedure is transformed into a work of art. Both in Heidegger's philosophy, and more especially in the Zen attitude to life, giving our full attention to ordinary daily activities, such as cleaning our shoes, sweeping the floor or making a cup of tea, is seen as a potential means of awakening us to the truth of how things are – the nature of Being.

Also, especially in his later thought, Heidegger adopts the idea that the achievement of authenticity requires *Gelassenheit,* which means the release from will and the abandonment of all effort. In Zen Buddhism (particularly in the *Soto* tradition) it is likewise maintained that enlightenment can never be willed but can only be cultivated by learning to 'let things be' in everyday life. Furthermore, Heidegger and Zen maintain that one cannot *resolve* to become enlightened or authentic. Nevertheless, each of them recommend a variety of procedures for placing one in a state whereby one is more likely to experience this non-willed letting go or release, that allows one to experience the truth of Being for the first time.

The parallels between Heidegger and Asian thought are clear. What is not certain is whether Heidegger was directly influenced by such thought, or whether this is merely an example of what has been called by some philosophers 'the universality of truth' expressing itself in a variety of ways.

Heidegger on Technology 8

One of the dominant themes of Heidegger's later writing is his critique of modern technology. Heidegger had never liked the modern cosmopolitan lifestyle with its consumerism, shallow values and disregard for nature, but from the late 1950s onwards this feeling intensified considerably. He wrote: 'Everywhere we remain unfree and chained to technology, whether we passionately affirm it or deny it.' He saw mankind in the grip of an obsession with production and profit – maximum yield at minimum cost, irrespective of the current or future consequences, and this calculating, mercenary behaviour governed all decisions. What most terrified Heidegger was his realization that these were only the very earliest symptoms of a 'diseased' way of thinking that set itself no limits – the certain prognosis being infinite technological expansion that would eventually eradicate all other ways of thinking. Human existence would eventually become completely subordinate to technological 'dictatorship'. He accurately predicted, nearly fifty years ago, that communication would be ruled by 'electronic thinking', with calculating machines circulating information.'

He observed the mesmerizing power of television as the most visible sign of the dominion of technology, and in a lecture commented: 'Human beings are, strictly speaking, no longer "at home" where, seen from outside, they live'. In other words, you may *appear* to be seated in your lounge but in fact, thanks to your television or video, you have been '*tele*ported' and are now a 'spectator' in a football stadium or perhaps the voyeur of an erotic sex scene. He saw this as an example of humanity's collective 'migration' into a condition of homelessness: 'Hourly and daily they are chained to radio and television … all that is already much closer to man today than his fields around his farmstead, closer than the conventions and customs of his village, than the tradition of his native world.'

Although Heidegger frequently expressed his preference for co-operating with nature, by using, for instance, windmills rather than nuclear power plants, what is of most importance to him in his discussion of technology, is *not* technology *itself*. He considered the debate over the atom bomb, for instance, as a mere 'journalistic footnote' to a crisis whose real source is rooted in 'the forgetting of Being'. This arose from the substitution of rationalistic scientific thinking for the insight of true penetration into the sense of Being, and resulted in 2000 years of egotistical philosophical thinking that has completely obscured our true relationship with Being. By looking at ourselves as some sort of 'thinking thing' we place ourselves – individually and collectively – at the centre of an existence that exists *for* us, and *because* of us. As Heidegger states: 'One type of being, the human being, believes that all of Being exists for it.' Heidegger saw the many physical expressions of technology as an inevitable outcome of this arrogant delusion, which is the *real* danger.

ENFRAMING: THE 'MIND-SET' OF TECHNOLOGY

The egocentric attitude of mankind gave rise to the 'mind-set' that not only underlies modern technological developments, but which also influences the way we approach virtually every other aspect of our lives. Heidegger called this attitude **Gestell** – which translates as **enframing**. Enframing describes our narrow, restricted understanding of ourselves and all things in existence in terms of 'resources' to be organized, enhanced, and exploited efficiently. This has resulted in our viewing the whole planet and all it contains as merely a vast stockpile of potential products available for extraction and manipulation for the benefit of our desires and goals, This misunderstanding has ruled our development since the time of Plato.

The process of 'enframing' seeks to make everything more accessible for utilization in the pursuit of our objectives, and thus motivates us to create the artifical boundaries that divide land into continents, countries, states, cities and communities. It causes us to define cultural and racial differences that allow us, when we are more powerful, to exploit those who 'are not like us'.

In addition, 'enframing' has inspired us to consider the creatures of our natural world mere *resources* for our use or entertainment – we make them 'homeless', abducting them from their primordial, essential contexts, and place them in zoos or in our own homes as exotic 'pets'. And the rest of existence is viewed in the same way. Trees, for instance, are viewed by this enframing state of mind as just a material resource for building houses, making furniture or producing paper. Or we see them as 'useful' because they absorb carbon dioxide and release oxygen to help us breathe, and their roots prevent erosion of the land in certain areas that would otherwise be uninhabitable.

Heidegger describes how this way of thinking has affected all of nature: 'Agriculture is now the mechanized food industry. Air is now set upon to yield nitrogen, the earth to yield ore, ore to yield uranium. Uranium is set upon to yield atomic energy. This setting-upon unlocks and exposes, driving to the maximum yield at minimum expense ... Nature has become a gigantic gasoline station, an energy source for modern technology and industry.'

In illustrating our enframing, technological attitude towards the earth, Heidegger describes how 'the dam across the living stream' is an 'enslavement' of the natural flow of the river in the service of turbines. Flora and fauna go to ruin in the inert reservoir behind the dam. He describes this as 'uncannily monstrous' – an example of *confrontation*, forceful *coercion* and harnessing of nature. In contrast he speaks of rural existence, when it *co-operates* with nature, as being a 'donation' (sowing), an 'acceptance' (harvest), a 'perennial custodianship' and restoration or 'renewal' of the earth.

Heidegger saw the enframing mind-set as evident not only in science and technology, but in every part of human existence, from atomic physics to the content of glossy magazines. We reveal its influence on our way of thinking in popular expressions such as 'the culture or leisure *industry*', or in horse racing as 'the racing *industry*', and in phrases like 'quality time'. Natural things are labeled 'natural resources' and human beings are called 'human resources'. Artworks and books are often viewed as 'information resources'. Even the act of writing is now called 'word-processing', suggesting that the very language we speak is regarded now as just another resource available for manipulation. Heidegger also observes enframing in the arts and sciences where teaching and research has been 'institutionalized' in terms of a predetermined area of enquiry that *dictates* and *precludes* various methods and topics. Education and research, rather than being an induction into a humanistic way of life, has been reduced to just another resource and object of consumption. He notes how this binding adherence to specific predetermined structures has degenerated the academic community into a collection of 'researchers' rather than 'genuine scholars'.

Consequently, for the 'enframed' technologically minded *Dasein*, *'to be'* simply means to be the manipulator and exploiter of other beings, or to be personally available for manipulation and exploitation.

Humans have been reduced to exploitable manpower or 'human resources', and everything else, even the moon and the planets, is viewed as 'stock' – an available supply of commodities or material resources. Even the 'human potential movement' is a symptom of this attitude of 'enframing' that is geared towards the total mobilization and enhancement of everything, *including* us. A piece of dialogue from the film *2001* epitomizes this current situation: when the robot computer HAL is asked if he is happy on the mission, he replies, 'I'm using all my capacities to the maximum. What more could a rational entity want?'

According to Heidegger, this outlook is destroying the intrinsic value or importance of everything around us, and to compensate for the resulting impoverished existence in which we now live, we desperately seek experiences in the form of superficial stimulation that leaves us fundamentally 'untouched'. So we consume never-ending quantities of entertainment and information and interact with *representations* of reality rather than reality itself – the epitome of this is seen in the virtual reality of the computer world.

Heidegger suggests that the ultimate purpose of all this manipulation of life is simply 'the will to will' – self-assertion for the sake of more power. We are gripped by the compulsion to control things. The destructive results of this surround us, and if we continue on this course, then our future could resemble the description expressed by author George Orwell's totalitarian ideologist: 'Power is not a means; it is an end ... if you want a picture of the future, imagine a boot stamping on a human face – forever.'

TECHNE, POIESIS AND THE ESSENCE OF TECHNOLOGY

In spite of this bleak outlook on the future, the problems of environmental destruction and the threat of nuclear war, Heidegger does not suggest taking any *practical* action for dealing with the negative effects of technology. Instead, he urges the necessity of approaching this question by reflecting on the *essence* of technology. He claimed that only an understanding of this essence can prepare us for an adequate response to the actual physical problems caused by modern technology.

Towards this end, Heidegger began researching all possible 'lost meanings' of the word 'technology'. The word originally derives from the ancient Greek **techne**, but since the 1830s it has come to mean 'the application of scientific knowledge and thinking to manufacturing'.

In its original sense as *techne*, it encompassed several possible meanings. It could mean the fine arts, the 'arts of the mind', the skills and activities of a craft worker, and it also contained a sense of what Heidegger called **poiesis** which means 'to bring into presence', or 'bring forth' – exactly what happens in all arts and crafts. According to Heidegger, this etymological research therefore indicates that *techne*, with its sense of *poiesis*, belongs to the realm of truth as *aletheia* – fundamental truth as unconcealment. So *techne*, in its original Greek meaning, includes connotations that have been omitted from our modern understanding and expression of technology. In its original sense, *techne* was not merely a practical aptitude or way of *making*, but more importantly a mode of knowing and revealing as the 'truth' of *aletheia*. That is why the word *techne* was used in reference to art, for the essence of art lies not in the act of making, but in the process of *disclosing the truth* – things as they really are.

Heidegger therefore concludes that technology, in its essence, 'is a mode of revealing' – a mode of fundamental truth, connected with the realm of *aletheia*.

He saw, however, that this original sense of *techne* had been lost with the with the fatal revolution of values that Heidegger ascribes to Plato's demeaning of entities and to the Aristotelian-Cartesian use of knowledge for the purpose of increasing mastery over nature. Consequently, though modern technology still 'discloses', it does so in a highly restricted manner that wipes out *poiesis* – the revealing of the 'presence' or 'being' of an entity.

The kind of revealing that occurs in modern technology is therefore very different from that which takes place in a work of art. Whereas art *allows* things to be revealed, technology obliges things to fulfill a *specific* purpose, things are 'disclosed' only within the framework of their particular type of usefulness. This mode of revealing, which is enframing, is the *essence* of modern technology.

ENFRAMING: DANGER OR SOURCE OF AWARENESS?

In a lecture on the dangers of the current age Heidegger claimed that 'the coming to presence of *enframing* is the (real) danger' For Heidegger, although enframing is the essence of technology, it is not *itself* anything technological or even a part of technology – it sustains technology, but exists independently from it. It is intrinsically connected with the world of technology, in that the technological outcome is what the mode of enframing itself demands. It is the logical and unavoidable consequence and conclusion of enframing. Theoretical science, as the most refined expression of enframing the world in terms of its calculability, unavoidably establishes the world as a resource for technological manipulation.

Heidegger wrote: 'it seems time and time again as though technology were a means in the hand of man. But in truth, it is the 'coming to presence' of man that is now being ordered forth to lend a hand to the 'coming to presence' of technology'.

We can see the truth of Heidegger's words in the rapid evolution of new computer technology, the supervision of genetic engineering research and also in new advances in atomic research. Mankind has been drawn into *serving* technology, thus 'lending a hand' to the coming to presence of technological developments. In so doing human beings are losing all contact with the deeper essence or meaning of their own Being.

As Heidegger understands it, because enframing is rooted in Being itself, in this sense it also *precedes* man – humans beings are not the *cause* of enframing, but rather an indispensible part of its expression. Enframing is clearly not something we *do,* since it already defines us and the world in which we live. We function within it – our actions are guided by it. Like a kind of destiny, it is happening to us, as a part of the mystery of existence. The essence of who we see ourselves to be is determined by enframing – we contribute to it, sustain it and expand its control over us – we are the primary resource of technology. For Heidegger therefore, the *essence* of technology is part of the question of the essence or meaning of Being. This is why Heidegger emphasizes that the dangers of the influence of enframing will remain, irrespective of the successes, failures or malign applications of technology.

Since the origin of enframing does not lie in any human act, but emerges as an expression of primordial Being, it must exist in the realm of truth. So where is the danger? Heidegger's response is that the action of revealing one facet of Being conceals others. Consequently, the view of existence provided by enframing automatically blocks our awareness of the remaining potential modes of Being. And since enframing is always the source of our world-view we remain *permanently* closed off from all these other ways of Being. The result, according to Heidegger, is that Being remains forever shrouded in oblivion – its deeper and richer meaning neglected and forgotten.

In the very fact that the process of enframing is rooted in Being lies the key to dealing with it – Heidegger expressed this in a line by his favourite poet Holderlin: 'Where danger is, grows also that which saves.' We can see clearly the truth of these words – it is enframing which brings our awareness to the danger of the oblivion of Being, which in turn directs us towards the question of Being. So, paradoxically, in the danger of enframing lies the potential motivation and source of our awareness of Being.

We can also see this seemingly paradoxical process at work in modern technology itself. In spite of the serious problems it is creating for our civilization and the whole planet, the solutions to these same problems appear to exist in their *source* – the science and technology that created them. After all, cleaner cars, energy-saving systems, wind farms, solar panels and other 'green' initiatives all depend on the *application* of science, rather than its rejection.

However, Heidegger points out that no matter how sophisticated our science, it will not be able to solve the difficulties caused by technology if we continue to view the planet through our 'enframed' way of thinking. We need first to reach a level of awareness where we see ourselves as 'custodians' rather than 'users' of the world in which we live.

So in spite of acknowledging the many successes of science and technology that have arisen as a result of this enframing perspective on existence, Heidegger points out that it is nevertheless an extremely limiting, one-sided and one-track approach to reality. Though the action of enframing allows us to develop a very valid type of practical and theoretical knowledge of the world, what is *not* valid is its false belief in its own totality. For enframing is definitely not the only kind of unconcealment contained in *techne*. There is also the way of unconcealment that is exemplified by a work of art and possibly by other means not yet considered. By viewing everything through this single filter of enframing, and mistaking this one-sided view of reality for 'omnicompetence' we live an impoverished existence that denies the rich variety of experience potentially available to us.

HEIDEGGER'S RESPONSE TO TECHNOLOGY

Heidegger considers that seeing technology as a problem for us to *fix* is yet *another* example of technological thinking. Instead of direct action, he believes the key to this dilemma may be found through reflective attunement to Being, which 'lets beings Be'. This 'letting-be' involves waiting and listening in an open receptive manner to the 'voice' of Being. He believed the answer might also be found in the creative arts, which are related to, and yet fundamentally different from, technology. Via their shared roots in *techne*, he saw art as perhaps capable of revealing a new, more 'poetic' form of technology.

Implied here seems to be the idea that if we simply allow ourselves to remain open to Being that there may arise an understanding of another way of Being that will spontaneously guide us in the right direction. This viewpoint is shared by many working within the field of **deep ecology**, who believe that saving the planet and all that it 'houses' requires a raising of consciousness; otherwise all direct action is taking place on unstable foundations that will ultimately crumble. The threat of technology, therefore, is not a problem that needs a *solution*, but an *ontological condition* that requires a transformation of our understanding of Being.

Heidegger's hope is not that we get rid of technology, but that we will achieve a healthier, 'free' relationship with it, based on an awareness and embracing of other ways of Being. He suggests that: 'We let technical devices enter our daily life, and at the same time leave them outside … as things which are nothing absolute but remain dependent upon something higher.'

He also recommends that we strive to protect the endangered 'species' of non-technological activities, which have now become **marginal practices** in our culture. He is referring to simple natural pleasures, such as genuine friendship, quiet walks through the countryside, sitting and gazing at the starlit sky – anything that is not motivated by the desire for 'productivity' or 'personal improvement'. He hoped this way of living might help establish a world in which non-technological practices were central and technology was marginal.

Interestingly, although Heidegger had no television set himself, he still watched sports on other people's sets – and though he detested the idea of using a typewriter to create his ideas and wrote all his texts by hand, he employed his brother to type them.

Frequently, our way of dealing with the damaging effects of technology does not focus on the source of the problem. The steps we take to protect nature are often themselves an expression of this same 'technological' attitude. For instance, we shout for laws to preserve the rainforests, whilst citing how they contain thousands of 'useful' natural products, such as possible cures for cancer. So even this worthy attempt to protect nature is entrapped within the same mind-set that it is fighting. The view of nature as a collection of natural 'resources' that exist for our benefit and the attempt to *control* and *manage* the situation are prime examples of our modern technological attitude to existence.

This is why Heidegger, controversially, thinks that even if we resolve all the negative expressions and consequences of technology, and use it only in 'positive' ways, the outcome *may* still be disastrous. The planet could be transformed potentially into a peaceful place, with nature perfectly controlled and providing food for everyone. Humans may achieve apparent 'harmonious satisfaction' with abundant entertainment offered by a plethora of pleasure-oriented hi-tech innovations. But Heidegger points out the very real danger here of becoming entrapped and entranced by such a lifestyle. In the process we are likely to lose all awareness of more meaningful and natural ways of living that allow us contact with the mystery of nature and the wonder of the meaning of Being. In the vice-like grip of our 'enframed', technological understanding of Being, we will mistakenly believe that this is all there is – life will have lost its depth, and we will have lost our true freedom.

In Heidegger's own words: 'The approaching tide of technological revolution in the atomic age could so captivate, bewitch, dazzle, and beguile man that calculative thinking may someday come to be accepted *as the only way* of thinking.'

FURTHER READING

The Cambridge Companion to Heidegger, edited by Charles Guignon, Cambridge University Press, 1999

Heidegger an Introduction, Richard Polt, University College London Press, 1999

The Later Heidegger, George Pattison, Routledge Philosophy Guidebooks, 2000

Martin Heidegger Basic Writings, edited by Farrell Krell, Routledge Press 2000

A Heidegger Dictionary, Michael Inwood, Blackwell Publishers Ltd, 2000

A Commentary on Heidegger's Being and Time (Revised Edition), Michael Gelven, Northern Illinois University Press, 1989

Martin Heidegger, George Steiner, The University of Chicago Press, 1999

GLOSSARY

aletheia Ancient Greek word for 'truth' – the root meaning is 'unconcealment'. Heidegger regarded truth as an 'uncovering' or 'disclosing' of what *is*.

anxiety The potentially enlightening, highly disturbing mood that bluntly confronts us with the constant possibility of our own death – the Nothingness that lies at the heart of human existence.

a priori Rudimentary knowledge or understanding that is pre-conceptual or innate.

as-structure The practical significance or purpose of a thing.

authentic The mode of existence in which *Dasein* has escaped the all-pervasive domination of ‹ ‹they-self' and is aware of its *own* self and its *own* possibilities. To be authentic therefore, is to be true to one's *own* self and to do one's *own* thing.

bauen German verb 'to build'. Heidegger replaced this sense of the word with the Old German usage which meant 'nurturing, cultivating, preserving and caring'.

beings (with a small 'b') A being (or beings) and its synonym *entity* (or *entities*) refers to events or things – animate or inanimate – that have an existence of some sort.

Being (with a capital 'B') is the 'existing' 'isness' or essence of beings (entities) – the primordial source of everything that exists in the universe.

Being-in-the-world Expresses *Dasein*'s innate comprehension of and indivisible unity with the *world* which is an intrinsic part of *Dasein*'s existence.

Being-with The social dimension of *Dasein*'s existence which is a fundamental feature of Being-in-the-world – directly or indirectly *Dasein* always and essentially experiences existence in relation to other people.

care The act of caring about our existence. Care is the basic feature in us that constitutes all our involvements in the world.

circumspection Describes the type of 'involved' (rather than detached or objective) 'looking around' one's environment that has a practical motive.

clearing The place in which Being reveals itself.

concern Means 'attending to' or 'taking care of' the way we handle 'ready-to-hand' things (computers, tools etc.) during the practical activities of our job and daily life.

conscience The primordial part of our consciousness that reminds us of our potential for living 'authentically'.

correspondence theory The standard definition of truth used today, in which judgements, statements or propositions are correct or true only if they factually 'match' the object or situation they are referring to. A proposition is either true or it is not.

Dasein Refers exclusively to human beings and their 'way of Being'. Used in place of the standard German terminology for *man* or *human being*. It can refer to a single human being as well as all human beings.

deep ecology The ecological movement that emphasizes raising mankind's consciousness as the primary means for saving the planet.

dualism the philosophical conception of reality as consisting of independently existing, principles or contrasting features, for instance, *mind* and *matter*.

enframing The technological 'mind-set' or attitude, which is characterized by a narrow, restricted understanding of ourselves and all things in existence as 'resources' for exploitation.

entity See 'beings'.

equipment A synonym for *ready-to-hand*.

Equipment totality The complete 'network' of entities in which a ready-to-hand item exists. All the components of this network are connected, or related, to each other in some way.

es weltet German phrase meaning 'it worlds' or 'it is worlding'.

Essence Heidegger's term 'essence' has nothing to do with the traditional idea of essence as a single, covering definition. His concept refers instead to 'that which makes something what it is' – in other words *Being*.

existential Each existential refers to a specific *a priori* mode of *Dasein*'s understanding and existence.

Existentialism Branch of philosophy which believes each individual has freedom of choice, and is therefore responsible for their own development and existence.

existenz Latin derivative meaning 'existence'.

facticity The sum total of our current situation and all our future possibilities which are the consequence of our *thrownness*.

fallenness The fundamental characteristic of inauthentic living as the *they-self* – defined by shallow, short-lived curiosity, empty talk or gossip and submission to the values, interpretations and interests of the anonymous general public.

fore-structure The web of significant relationships that define the existence of a ready-to-hand entity – an awareness of the fore-structure is involved in all interpretation.

fundamental ontology The term used by Heidegger to emphasize his unique approach to ontology, which investigates exclusively the nature of Being *itself* rather than the entities or *ontical* features of existence that have been the focus of earlier 'erroneous' approaches to ontology.

Gestell (The German word for 'enframing'.) *See* 'enframing'.

ground The foundation or 'basis of'.

guilt Our primordial existential guilt which arises from the knowledge that our existence is rooted in Nothingness, and that we can never be all that we can be.

inauthentic The normal way we live (as the 'they-self') which is characterized by a lack of awareness of our *own* self and our *own* possibilities due to an absorption in ways of living provided by others.

interpretation The seeing of things in their *completion* rather than in terms of their *characteristics*.

irresoluteness Refers to *Dasein*'s mindless absorption in the present as the 'they-self', in which it is ignorant of its *own* self and its *own* future possibilities.

logos Heidegger's term for a language in which the words are inseparable from what they name. He saw Greek as such a language: 'Through the audible Greek word we are directly in the presence of the thing itself, not first in the presence of a mere word-sign.'

marginal practices Non-technological activities that are not motivated by the desire for 'productivity' or 'personal improvement'.

metaphysics Philosophical study of the fundamental principles of existence, such as substance, time, space etc.

meaning Our understanding of the function of something, which includes its involvement in a network of significant purposive relationships with other entities.

moods To be in a mood refers to being 'tuned into' life in a certain way that influences our general attitude towards the totality of things – this determines the nature of our understanding at any given moment.

nihilism Branch of philosophy which denies that human existence has any significance at all.

ontic Refers to things in existence and their characteristics without regard for the primordial fact of their Being (existence).

ontic truth Refers to truth that has been 'proven' by tangible 'facts'.

ontological Information, remarks, questions or observations pertaining to Being itself or the Being of entities.

ontological difference Refers to the fundamental distinction or dissimilarity between *Being* and *beings*.

ontologist Philosopher who investigates the nature of Being.

ontology The philosophy of Being (or branch of Metaphysics) which focuses specifically on Being itself, or the Being of entities.

onto-theology Any philosophical approach that searches for an *origin* of Being in some type of substance or transcendental super-Being (God).

parousia The ancient Greek word for 'Being' and also 'substance'.

poiesis Ancient Greek that means 'to bring into presence', or 'bring forth'.

present-at-hand entities Describes entities for which *Dasein* has no use, or alternatively, merely detached, objective interest.

primordial That which is prior to everything – which has existed from the beginning and therefore cannot be derived from anything else.

ready-to-hand entities Entities that are experienced by *Dasein* as having a useful, practical function for human purposes. Relating to things as 'ready-to-hand' is *Dasein*'s fundamental way of Being-in-the-world.

resoluteness The key feature of authenticity which describes *Dasein*'s total commitment to the fundamental path it has *freely* chosen in life. Resoluteness requires a clear perspective of the totality of one's existence and the constant possibility of death.

Sein The original German term for 'Being' which is derived from the verb 'to be'.

Seyn The archaic German spelling of *Sein* ('Being').

solicitude Taking care of or providing for the welfare of those in need of help.

techne The ancient Greek from which the word 'technology' derives. It encompassed several meanings: the fine arts, the 'arts of the mind' and the skills and activities of a craft worker.

technology The application of scientific knowledge and thinking to manufacturing.

temporality 'Existing within time' – refers to our fundamental way of Being which simultaneously spans, and is constituted by, the three dimensions of time.

they-self The inauthentic mode of the self in which one lives according to the particular range of social and cultural customs, expectations and interpretations of life offered by the 'world' one inhabits. From birth onwards most of us live our complete lives as the 'they-self'.

thrownness The event of being thrust into an existence not of our choice that has been determined by the random forces of chance or destiny. Our thrownness ultimately determines all aspects of our existence.

understanding *Dasein*'s *a priori* (innate) rudimentary understanding of its everyday world, the things in it and how it fits into this world. This pre-conceptual comprehension of existence is a fundamental feature of *Dasein*'s being-in-the-world.

unready-to-hand Refers to the present-at-hand condition of ready-to-hand items that are broken or rendered unusable.

world The entire circumstances or *context* of *Dasein*'s life – e.g. birthplace, country of residence, culture, social environment, education, family, friends, career etc.

worldhood Refers to the underlying infrastructure of a *Dasein*'s world – in other words, the totality of all our practical and functional relationships with everything in the particular world we inhabit.

INDEX

a priori structure of
  Dasein 25–6
  Dasein's being in
    the world 27
abandonment 75
academic career 3–7
'afterlife' 50
aletheia 62–3
  containing
    unconcealment
    and concealment
    65
always already 33
Anaximander 10
Ancient Greek 68–9
  aletheia 62
Anglo–American
  philosophy 6
Angst 20
anxiety 43–6, 54
  and death 51
Arendt, Hannah 5
argument against
  Heidegger's
  approach 12–13
Aristotle 4, 10
artefacts 29
as-structure 42–3
atom bomb 80
authenticity 54–60
  authentic self 34

awareness of
  inauthenticity 38
  and self-fulfilment
    57

banality 27
being 11
  Dasein as way of
    being 24
  questioning the
    meaning of 13
  'being' and 'Being'
    14–15
being and time
  24–48
Being and Time
  5–6, 18–19
  ontology in 11–12
being-in-the-world
  27, 33–4, 68
  moods 40
being-toward-death
  49–53, 57–8
being-with-others
  32–3
beingness 16
Big Bang theory 21
Brentano, Franz 2

calculative thinking
  89
cancer 88
care 46–8
  caring 47

guilt as care 55
central concepts of
  Being and *Time*
  24–48
circumspection 28
clearing 15, 63–4
  complex area of
    possibilities 65
coercion 81
Coleridge, Samuel 23
computers 85
concealment 64–5
concern 28
confrontation 81
conscience, guilt and
  authenticity
  54–60
correspondence
  theory 63
counter-culture 35
creative arts 87

Dasein 21, 24–48,
  67–8
  Da-sein 26, 68
  structure of 25–6
  see also Sein
De-Nazification
  Commission 8
death 49–53
  authentic awareness
    of 52–3
  'facts of life' and
    50–1

deep ecology 87
Der Spiegel 8
Descartes, René 4
destiny 33
detachment 57
Dilthey, Wilhelm 3
Dostoyevsky,
    Fyodor 3

education of
    Heidegger 2–3
egotism 80
enframing 80–7
    and unconcealment
    86–7
enlightenment 73,
    75–6
entertainment 88–9
Epicurus 49
equipment 28
'equipment totality'
    29–31
equiprimordial
    features 46
Ereignis 73
essence 14–15
    of technology 83–4
everyday existence
    27–8
everyday language
    66–7
existence 12
existentialism 6
existentials 26

exploitation 82

facticity 33
'facts of life' and
    death 50–1
fallenness 36–7
falling 35–8
    and inauthenticity
    35–6
finitude 56
fore–conception 43
fore–having 43
fore–sight 43
fore–structure 42
free choice 58
fundamental
    ontology 12

Gandhi, Mahatma 58
Gelassenheit 77
genetic engineering
    85
German 68–9
God 11, 13
green initiatives 86
guilt 54–60

Hawking, Stephen 22
hearing 71
Hegel, Georg 4
Heidegger's
    fundamental
    ontology 11–12
Heraclitus 10

Hitler, Adolf 5, 7, 58
    see also Nazism
Hölderlin, Johann
    74, 96
Holocaust 8
horizon 17
human potential
    movement 82
Husserl, Edmund 3,
    5, 11, 24

ideolect 72
idle curiosity 36
inauthenticity 34–48
    and death 51
    and falling 35–6
    structure of
    authenticity 38
indifference 36
initial subject-matter
    of the enquiry
    15–17
interpretation 42–3
intrinsic value 82–3
introspection 32
irresoluteness 58–9
'isness' 14–15

Kant, Immanuel 4,
    24
Kierkegaard, Sören 3

language 61–72
    Heidegger's

concept of 66
language of being
    67–8
Latin 68
lethe 65
life of Heidegger 1–9
light 14
logos 68

manipulation 82, 85
meaning 43
meaning of life
    10–23
meaninglessness 13
    abyss of 37
means-end
    approach 37
metaphysics 6, 20
moods 38–41
mortality 50
    see also death
music 40–1

Nazism 7–8
    see also Hitler,
    Adolf
near-death
    experience 52
network 29
Nietzsche, Friedrich 3
nihilism 13
not-ness 55
nothing 6, 19–21

and non-sense 20
nothingness 44
something rather
    than nothing
    21–2
nothingness 44
nuclear power
    stations 80

objectivity 12, 27
omnicompetence 87
ontic investigation 15
ontic knowledge 10
ontic truth 63
onto-theology 11
ontological
    difference 15
ontological truth 63
ontology 3, 10–11
    ontological 'error'
    of Western
    philosophy 11
    understanding of
    death 52
Orwell, George 83

Parmenides 10
parousia 11
phenomenology 3–5
Plato 4, 10–11, 61, 80
    demeaning of
    identities 84
poetry 71–2

'poiesis' 83
present–at–hand
    28–9
preservation 88
primary access to
    being 70
primordial 11
    and moods 38
projection 33–4, 70
propositional truth
    63
pure consciousness
    11

ready-to-hand 28–9,
    31, 42
reality 82–3
resoluteness 58–9
resonance 73
response to nihilism
    13

Sartre, Jean–Paul 6
Sein 14, 67
    language of being
    67–8
    see also Dasein
significance of
    unanswerable
    questions 22–3
silent 'saying' 70–1
    and hearing 71
Socrates 76

solicitude 47
space and time 31
substance 11
suicide 52
supreme being 11

talk 69–70
  access to being 70
  inauthentic 36
Tao Te Ching 73–4
taoism, Zen and
    Heidegger 73–8
'techne' 83–4
technology 79–89
television 79, 88
temporality 18
the they 34
they–self 34–5
  anxiety 45
thinking subject 11
thrownness 33–4
  anxiety 45
time as the horizon
    of being 17–18
traditional concepts
    of truth 61–2
truth 61–72
  Heidegger's truth
    of aletheia 62–5
  philosophy as
    search for 61
  traditional
    concepts of 61–2

truth of 'aletheia' and
    language 61–72

unanswerable
    questions 22–3
unconcealment 62–3
  degrees of 65
  poiesis 83–4
understanding 41–2
Universal Being 23
universality of truth
    78
unready-to-hand 29
untruth 64

vision 14
vocabulary 13

'with-world' 32
world 26–7
worldhood 27, 30

R' Dine